BICYCLING.
MAGAZINE'S

New Cyclist Handbook

Ride with Confidence and Avoid Common Pitfalls

EDITED BY ED PAVELKA

RODALE

Cover and Interior Designer: Susan P. Eugster
Cover Photographer: Kurt Wilson
Interior Photographers: Gregg Adams, Mel Lindstrom, Paul Schraub

Library of Congress Cataloging-in-Publication Data

    Bicycling magazine's new cyclist handbook : ride with confidence and avoid common pitfalls / edited by Ed Pavelka.
        p.   cm.
    Includes index.
    ISBN 1–57954–251–4 paperback
    1. Cycling.   2. Cycling—Equipment and supplies.   I. Title: New cyclist handbook.   II. Pavelka, Ed.   III. Bicycling.
    GV1041 .B529   2000
    796.6—dc21   00–037262

Distributed to the book trade by St. Martin's Press

2   4   6   8   10   9   7   5   paperback

Visit us on the Web at www.rodalesportsandfitness.com, or call us toll-free at (800) 848-4735.

WE **INSPIRE** AND **ENABLE** PEOPLE TO IMPROVE
THEIR LIVES AND THE WORLD AROUND THEM

Notice

The information in this book is meant to supplement, not replace, proper road cycling and mountain biking training. Like any sport involving speed, equipment, balance, and environmental factors, cycling poses some inherent risk. The editors and publisher advise readers to take full responsibility for their safety and know their limits. Before practicing the skills described in this book, be sure that your equipment is well-maintained, and do not take risks beyond your experience, aptitude, training, and comfort level.

Contents

PART FOUR

Body Care

PART FIVE

Bicycle Care

Introduction

Your new bike comes with one very essential accessory—the owner's manual supplied by the manufacturer. It tells you all about your particular model. That's important, but to really know how to ride well, you need much more information. That's where this book comes in.

You're holding the best collection of expert advice and tips available for new riders. It was written with one goal in mind—to give you the knowledge that will help you avoid common mistakes and get more enjoyment on your bike from the very first ride.

Pay special attention to the chapters on setting up your road riding and mountain biking positions. A good position is essential for efficiency as well as comfort and confidence. Other chapters introduce you to riding techniques that are easy to master, helping you develop solid skills and good habits from the start.

Before long, you'll be looking for ways to test your growing ability. One of the best is cycling's 100-mile challenge of endurance and determination—the century ride. When the bug bites, use the training program in chapter 15 and have the time of your life.

Finally, there's a special section on how to keep your new bike working as well as it did the day you wheeled it from the shop. Use the easy step-by-step maintenance procedures in chapters 21 and 22, and you may find that caring for your bike is almost as much fun as riding it.

Welcome to cycling! See you on the roads and trails.

PART ONE

Starting Out

Choose the Right Bike

In the 1990s, nearly 75 percent of all adult bicycles purchased were mountain bikes. This is like saying that three-quarters of all new car buyers are driving away in sport-utility vehicles. It's a striking statistic, especially when you consider that, like autos, there are many other types of bikes. Making it even more remarkable is the fact that most of these mountain bikes are never ridden on anything but pavement. So why are so many people buying them?

Perhaps it's peer pressure or herd mentality—keeping up with friends or the neighbors. Maybe it's a lifestyle decision—mountain biking has become cycling's "cool" image. It could be simple impulse—you need a way to exercise, and mountain bikes beckon because you see them everywhere. Or it could be the attraction of rugged durability and a comfortable upright riding position.

Nothing is gained by knocking these reasons. After all, anything that attracts people to cycling should be applauded. But because there are different types of bikes for different purposes, a mountain bike may not be the best choice for everyone—or even for 75 percent of everyone. If you buy the type of bike that matches your reason for riding, you'll be happier and stay with the sport longer.

How can you reach the right decision? The first step is to decide which features are advantageous for your type of riding and which could actually work against it. To help, here's a checklist.

1. Consider your goals in cycling. Do you imagine yourself winning a race? Commuting to work? Exploring backcountry trails? Will you use your new bike for weekend touring, bike club outings, or daily rides for exercise? Once you pin it down, talk with like-minded people and learn what type of bike works best for them. (You can meet them through your local bike club or shop.) They may even let you give their bikes a try. Ideally, you'll be able to experience the attributes of the three main types: road, mountain, and hybrid or crossbikes, which combines features of both. You can also take test rides at bike shops that offer them.

2. Ponder the riding possibilities in your area. Are you blessed with miles of scenic, lightly traveled paved roads? Is there a network of dirt roads or trails? Safe bike lanes for traveling on city streets? You'll ride more and heighten your cycling enjoyment if you get a bike that lets you take advantage of your area's best opportunities.

3. Analyze your personality and tendencies. Are you a win-at-all-costs athlete rather than the fun-oriented, recreational type? Do you put a premium on having the latest technology? Are you forever tinkering and upgrading things you buy? If you answer yes to these questions, you'll be happiest with a top-of-the-line model. Or are you a person who probably won't notice a bike's components until something goes wrong, and then you'll take it to a shop for service? If so, basic equipment will suffice and protect your budget as well.

Model Selection

Here's a rundown on all the types of adult bikes that you'll find when visiting most large bike shops. Use it to choose the machine that's best for your needs.

Road Racers

These are cycling's thoroughbreds. Their drop handlebars promote a low, aerodynamic posture for greater speed with less effort, while offering the widest range of hand positions for comfort. The narrow rims and tires are lighter and more efficient than those found on mountain bikes or hybrids. The gear range, with two chainrings instead of three, is both narrower and higher, which improves pedaling efficiency.

Pros: Its light weight aids climbing and handling; offers a thrilling ride; ideal bike for fast recreational cycling as well as racing.

Cons: Relatively delicate frame and components; skinny tires are more susceptible to punctures; fewer hill-leveling low gears; new cyclists may need time to adapt to the riding position.

Touring/Sport Road Bikes

This type resembles a road racer except for a slightly longer frame and lower gears, achieved with triple chainrings like those on hybrids and mountain bikes. Wheels are relatively light with medium-width tires so the bike rolls efficiently, helped by the advantages of a drop bar. The frame has threaded fittings called eyelets to assist installation of fenders and racks for touring or commuting.

Pros: Good load-carrying capacity; wide gear range; longer wheelbase for softer ride and autopilot steering; light enough for performance riding; some accessories may be included.

Cons: Heavier than a road racer; handling not as snappy.

Mountain Bikes

They're being used for everything—trail riding, off-road racing, commuting, touring, recreational cruising. Though in existence only since the early 1980s, mountain bikes are by far the biggest sellers of all adult two-wheelers.

Pros: Comfortable upright riding position (though racing models have become long and low); fat shock-absorbent and flat-resistant tires; suspension forks and frames for improved control and comfort; convenient shift and brake levers; strong frame, fork, and wheels; low gears for easy climbing; plenty of load-carrying capacity; many have low-maintenance, sealed-bearing components.

Cons: Upright riding position and wide, soft, knobby tires make for slower and tougher pedaling on pavement; usually several pounds heavier than a comparably priced road bike; limited hand positions make long rides less comfortable; extra maintenance for suspension.

Hybrids

Here's what you get when you combine a road and mountain bike, using the latter's riding position and low gearing, and the former's lighter wheels with narrower tires. Hybrids are also known as cross bikes.

Pros: Fine commuting bike; can handle unpaved roads and smooth trails; good resistance to flats, thanks to thicker, dual-purpose tires; rolls easier on pavement than most mountain bikes; good load-carrying capacity; many available with suspension seatposts, stems, or forks.

Cons: Upright riding position catches wind; usually heavier than comparably priced road bike; flat handlebar limits hand positions; less suited for off-road rigors than a mountain bike, but slower on pavement than a road bike.

City/Cruiser/Comfort Bikes

More common in Europe than in North America, this bike is designed to make urban or neighborhood transportation convenient. It provides a comfortable upright riding position like a hybrid, often using a wide, upswept handlebar. It may have low-maintenance features such as a drivetrain with gears built into the rear hub, a chainguard, and fenders. Lights, racks, and a kickstand may be included. Pedals are usually rubber without clips or straps.

Pros: Cool retro styling like bikes from the 1950s; medium-width tires are flat-resistant; good load-carrying capacity; fenders and chainguard keep you cleaner in wet weather; long wheelbase provides soft ride; internal gears can be shifted while you're stopped; low maintenance.

Cons: The many helpful features add weight, making climbing more difficult; upright riding position and wide tires reduce speed; one-speed or internal hub gearing not sufficient for hilly terrain.

Recumbents

Named for their reclined-rider position, recumbents are more popular than ever, thanks to lower prices and greater publicity about their benefits.

Pros: No strain on hands, buttocks, neck, or shoulders because you're pedaling in laid-back, chairlike comfort; full back support; fun, go-cart feel; convenient controls; the fastest type of bike on descents and in flat terrain (even faster with a windshield, an option on some models).

Cons: Takes practice to master; most are heavier and slower on climbs than conventional bikes; some are tricky to transport because of their length.

Tandems

This category is growing, too, thanks to lower prices and more companies producing models. Tandems are the great equalizer—the perfect way to keep two riders of different abilities together, such as a husband and wife or a parent and child. They also let two equally matched cyclists see what their combined horsepower can do. Tandems come in road, mountain, or recumbent versions.

Pros: Generally faster than a single bike; great stability at speed; promotes conversation, helping long distances pass quicker; the rider in back (stoker) is free to read maps, listen to a personal stereo, or make lunch.

Cons: Takes practice for riders to become coordinated; stoker is susceptible to unexpected impacts transmitted through the rear wheel; difficult to transport; hard on equipment, particularly wheels; slower on climbs; mountain tandems work great on fire trails but are limited on singletrack.

Be a Smart Shopper

Once you have the best type of bike pinned down, use the following tips when hunting for the exact bike to buy.

Carefully check the fit. For road bikes, you should be able to stand over the top tube and still have an inch or two of clearance to your crotch. For hybrids or cruisers, this should be 2 to 3 inches, especially if you'll ride it on unpaved terrain where sudden dismounts are more likely. For mountain bikes, the gap should be 3 inches or more. In other words, your correct mountain bike frame size (seat-tube length) will be about 3 inches smaller than that of your ideal road bike frame. Lacking a bike to straddle, stand barefoot and have someone measure from your crotch to the floor. Subtract 10 to 11 inches for your approximate road bike size, and 13 to 14 inches for your mountain bike size. A hybrid falls between. A more precise calculation isn't necessary because a bike's seat and handlebar are adjustable to make the fit just right, as explained in chapters 4 and 5. Recumbents generally fit a much wider range of riders than can a conventional bike of a given size. For this reason, few recumbents are offered in different frame sizes.

Consider suspension. Shock-eating forks, stems, seatposts, and frames can be found on all three main bike types. Generally, suspension adds cost and weight and may increase maintenance slightly. It's invalu-

Bike Buyer's Checklist

Finally, the big day has come—you're heading down to the bike shop to take possession of your brand new rig. Here are eight things to remember before you seal the deal.

- ☐ Make sure it's the exact model, color, and size you want. Be sure components were exchanged, or accessories installed, as you ordered.
- ☐ Have your riding clothes and shoes so it's easy to accurately adjust the seat and handlebar.
- ☐ Spin the wheels to make sure they're true and the brakes don't rub.
- ☐ Be sure the tires are inflated to the manufacturer's recommended pressure.
- ☐ If you're uncertain, ask to be shown how the quick-releases work on the brakes and hubs. Remove and reinstall a wheel several times to become familiar with the procedure.
- ☐ Learn how to remove slack from the gear and brake cables using the barrel adjusters.
- ☐ Before heading for home, go for a short test ride to make sure everything is working properly.
- ☐ Ask about the free 30-day checkup that most shops provide, and don't forget the owner's manual. Read it thoroughly prior to your first real ride.

able, however, for aggressive off-road riding because it keeps the wheels on the ground and softens impacts, dramatically improving control and comfort. For these reasons, suspension has become standard on serious mountain bikes and can be retrofitted to older models. For road riding, suspension is much less vital, but it will add comfort if most of the pavement in your area has seams, ripples, cracks, or patches.

Limit your shopping. It's wise to check different bike stores, but it's possible to overdo it and then become paralyzed by indecision or buy on a whim because you're weary. If you still can't decide after test-riding two bikes that are similar in cost and equipment, it's fine to make the decision in favor of the shop that simply gives you the most help and best feeling.

When budgeting, include the cost of any accessories or upgrades. Usually, it's cheaper to buy these as part of a new-bike package rather than piecemeal. This is especially true for equipment swaps, such as when going from standard to clipless pedals. Make the deal when the parts you don't want are still brand new.

Realize that big discounts are unlikely. Although you may find certain models on sale (usually at season's end), few shops can afford to slash prices. In fact, the average markup on bikes is minimal compared to that of almost every other retail business. Hidden costs reduce profits and force dealers to demand full price. For example, bikes must be assembled, have high shipping costs, and usually come with a free tune-up after the sale. So instead of haggling over the bike price, ask if it's possible to get a discount on accessories. The markup on these items is higher, so some shops will work with new bike buyers.

Take a test ride. This is still the best way to judge a bike. Make sure the tires are fully inflated, the seat is adjusted for your leg length, and the handlebar height is right. If the bike has suspension, have the salesperson set it for your body weight. Wear the same clothes and shoes that you're used to riding in or will be riding in. Once on the road, shift and brake repeatedly. Climb and descend a hill. Make turns. If you're testing a suspended bike, find rough surfaces so that you can feel the shocks in action. Ride for as long as it takes to get a good impression of the bike. By testing two or three bikes this way, one should emerge as the clear winner.

2

Clothing and Accessories

When you're budgeting for a new bike, be sure to set aside some money for accessories. All of the following items will improve your cycling experience. They're prioritized and approximate prices are listed to help you choose wisely. Included are things you "must have" for safe, enjoyable riding; those you "should have" to increase comfort, speed, or convenience; and those that are "nice to have" if you can afford them.

Must Have

Helmet ($30 to $150). Modern expanded-polystyrene helmets are light, cool, and stylish. Two innovations have become popular: a detachable visor to shield your face against sun, rain, mud, and branches, and a lightweight "locking" device that extends from the rear of the helmet to hug the back of your head, providing a firmer fit. Check for a safety certification sticker inside to be sure that the helmet meets current standards. (All of those from the major companies do.) If you have a helmet that is several years old, be aware that manufacturers say foam is slowly degraded by sunlight, sweat, air pollution, and general wear and tear. The result is that the foam becomes less able to absorb impacts. Consider buying a new helmet that is also likely to fit better and have superior ventilation.

Water bottle and cage ($7 to $15). The cardinal rules of hydration are to drink before you're thirsty and to down at least 22 ounces every hour. Most frames have mounts for two cages, so if you sweat a lot or ride for more than 60 minutes at a time, buy a pair.

Flat repair kit ($10 to $15). Sooner or later, you'll get a flat tire, so you need to carry the necessary repair items. Your kit should include tire levers for removing the tire, a tube that matches your valve type and tire size, and a tube patch kit. Add two pieces of canvas for covering large slits or holes in a tire casing from the inside.

Seatbag ($10 to $20). Choose a seatbag that is big enough to hold your flat repair kit and whatever else you like to carry (phone card, ID, keys, energy bar, all-in-one tool, emergency money). Some models have zippers that expand their capacity—great for stowing that windbreaker when the day warms up.

Frame-fit pump ($20 to $30). Buy a pump of the proper length to wedge securely under your frame's top tube or in front of the seat tube. Make sure it has the correct end to fit your valves (Schrader, like those on car tires, or the narrow presta type). Some chucks convert to either. Also consider a minipump. Models start as low as $10. These are less than half the length of frame-fit pumps and mount to clips that go under a bottle cage. A minipump doesn't inflate tires as quickly as a frame-fit pump, but it's lighter and more portable. You can easily carry it with you when you leave your bike.

Chain lube ($5 to $8). Use a spray or drip lube regularly to reduce drivetrain wear and noise and to keep shifts quick and smooth. Wipe excess lube from the chain so it doesn't fling onto the frame or rear wheel or act as a dirt magnet.

Should Have

Lock ($15 to $40). Relatively expensive U-locks offer the best security, but they're heavy and require removing the front wheel. Lower-cost cables with padlocks are sufficient for occasional use in low-risk areas. If you plan to lock your bike frequently in public places, consider purchasing both a U-lock and a cable lock, and use them in tandem. Always lock your bike to an immovable object, not just to itself. Make sure the bike can't be lifted up and off. Be certain the lock encloses both wheels as well as the frame.

Headlight ($15 to $250) and reflective material ($5 to $15). All states require lights after dark. For frequent night riding, consider a premium dual-beam rechargeable headlight. For occasional evening rides, especially on roads with streetlights, a less expensive light that runs on regular batteries will do. For either type of headlight, use a battery-powered taillight ($10 to $20) that clamps to the seatpost. Apply reflective tape to your frame, helmet, crankarms, pedals, and rims, and consider a reflective vest ($15).

Tool kit or all-in-one tool ($15 to $40). Your tool kit should include flat-head and Phillips screwdrivers, a small adjustable wrench or sockets, allen wrenches, a chain rivet extractor, and a spoke wrench. Keep it in your seatbag.

Gloves ($15 to $35). For road riding, gloves that have half-fingers and padded palms increase comfort and reduce abrasions in a crash. For mountain biking, there are more protective models that have full fingers or three-quarter fingers with a full thumb. Choose gloves with terry cloth on the thumb or back so you can wipe your nose or eyes during rides.

Shorts ($25 to $110). Your riding comfort goes way up when sitting on a soft, absorbent pad ("chamois") with no irritating seams. In general, the greater the number of panels (up to eight) that are used to make the shorts, the better the fit and the higher the price. Also increasing cost is a built-in bib top. For those who don't want traditional skintight black spandex, the same pads are available inside loose-fitting, casual-looking baggy shorts.

Shoes ($50 to $250). The soles of road shoes are extra-stiff to prevent foot pain and numbness from pedal pressure and to transfer more of your power to turning the crankset. Touring and mountain bike shoes have ridged or knobby soles that can be walked in fairly comfortably. Shoes with cleats that snap into the pedals offer the best power link, but they are more awkward for walking unless the cleats are recessed into the soles (as they are in most mountain bike shoes).

Eyewear ($15 to $110; more for prescription lenses). Sunglasses stop airborne debris and ultraviolet (UV) radiation. Wraparound models made specifically for cycling are impact-resistant and interfere less with peripheral vision than sunglasses with conventional frames. Some models offer interchangeable lenses of different colors, including clear for night riding. A rearview mirror ($10) that attaches to your glasses or helmet is another handy vision aid, especially if you're a commuter.

Clipless pedals ($40 to $180). Pedals without clips improve riding efficiency because the shoe cleat snaps into the pedal, allowing you to pull up and back rather than just push down. (They're called clipless because they eliminate the need for traditional toeclips and straps.) They also hold your feet in the correct position and prevent them from slipping off. Clipless pedals work like ski bindings, releasing your feet in the event of a fall. Most models let your feet pivot freely, or float, several degrees before they pop out. This reduces the risk of knee strain.

Nice to Have

Floor pump ($25 to $60). Good floor pumps inflate tires much faster than frame-fit pumps, and have built-in gauges that display pressure. Use a floor pump at home and save your frame-fit pump for emergency flat repairs so that it will last.

Cyclecomputer ($20 to $90). Most cyclecomputers will tell you the current speed, average speed, maximum speed, trip distance, and ride time. Fancier models include features such as cadence, altitude, temperature, or heart rate. Some are backlit for night riding, and some are wireless (no cord between the wheel sensor and handlebar-mounted monitor).

Jersey ($20 to $75). The cycling-specific jersey has three rear pockets for carrying things like food, maps, or extra clothing. It also fits snugly to reduce wind drag, wicks perspiration to keep you drier and cooler, and should have bright colors to make you more noticeable on the road. A long zipper in front helps you regulate the air hitting your chest as the temperature rises or falls.

Rear rack ($25 to $50). A rack is a good idea if you frequently carry things that won't fit into a jersey pocket or seatbag. You can strap large items to the rack or put them in a rack trunk ($30 to $75). If your frame doesn't have eyelets for attaching a rack, use one that clamps to the seatpost.

Fenders ($25 to $40). Plastic fenders keep you and your bike cleaner when you ride on wet roads or muddy trails.

Car rack ($50 to $300). You may need a car rack if you can't use the best way to get your bike from here to there—riding it. A car rack means no more stuffing your rig into the trunk or backseat. Trunk-mounted racks are cheaper and don't require lifting the bike over your head, but they block access and they leave bikes more vulnerable to tampering or accidents. Roof-mounted models hold more bikes, prevent scratches, and keep the trunk clear. But watch out for low overhangs. You can also find racks that attach to a bumper, trailer hitch, external spare tire, or inside a van or pickup bed.

Winter wear. If you want to be a year-round rider, you'll need this cold-weather gear: tights ($40 to $100); full-finger gloves ($15 to $60); a cap, balaclava, or wide headband ($10 to $30) that fits under your helmet; a vented jacket with wind-resistant panels on the chest and arms ($50 to $150); and booties ($20 to $60) to protect your feet from frigid wind and water.

3

For Women Only

Not long ago, there wasn't much to bike sizing for women. A woman bought any frame that was not too big to stand over. She rode bent forward like the guys, and if it hurt, well, it hurt. She could switch to a shorter stem to ease the ache in her back, but that was about the only concession that could be made. When female riders complained of seat or neck or shoulder pain, the common reply was, "You'll get used to it."

Some did and some didn't. All women aren't built alike—and they're certainly not built like men. According to Andrew Pruitt, Ed.D., director of the Boulder Center for Sports Medicine in Boulder, Colorado, most women have a proportionately shorter torso and longer legs than men, plus a wider pelvis and less upper-body strength. Dr. Pruitt knows cyclists and their fitting problems because he has worked for years with U.S. national team riders at the Olympic Training Center in Colorado Springs. Even if a bike fits a woman's leg length, its top tube, stem, or crankarms might be too long and its saddle could be too narrow.

So what happens if your bike doesn't fit right?

If you ride only a couple of miles around the neighborhood, probably nothing, says Dr. Pruitt. But if you crank up the mileage, you can experience back, neck, hip, or buttocks pain in varying degrees of severity. And your pedaling efficiency can suffer just as much. Thankfully, these problems are now well-understood, and more manufacturers are answering the need for bikes that fit women better. These are some of their considerations.

Frame. Because of their proportionately shorter torsos, women usually need a shorter top tube. But if the rider is quite small—under 5-foot-4— the top tube can be so short that it brings the front wheel too close. This causes her feet to overlap the wheel when either one is fully forward in the pedal stroke. The result can be contact and a crash during slow riding when the wheel might be turned sharply. Some manufacturers resolve this problem by using a smaller-diameter front wheel. Georgena Terry, founder of Terry Precision Cycling for Women, is a leader in this area. Her company makes its smaller road bikes with a 24-inch front wheel and a standard 700C wheel in back. This trick also allows these bikes to retain a relatively normal head-tube angle for proper steering behavior.

It's also important to have the correct seat angle to ensure that your saddle (and subsequently your legs) is in the correct fore/aft position above the crankset. (Moving your seat back and forth enables you to fine-tune this.) Generally, people with longer thighs need a 72- or 73-degree seat angle, and shorter-thighed folks do better with a slightly steeper angle that moves them farther forward over the crankset.

Stem. The oldest trick in the book is to compensate for an overly long top tube by installing a stem with a shorter forward extension. This brings the handlebar closer to the seat. Several manufacturers make very short stems. Your local bike shop can order one for you if it's not in stock.

Handlebar. Women's shoulders tend to be narrower than men's. A bar that is right for a guy may be too wide for you and cause pain in the shoulders, upper back, and neck. Terry offers 36- and 38-cm drop-style road handlebars to more precisely correspond to a woman's shoulder width (measured from bony end to bony end). Most flat handlebars found on mountain bikes and hybrids can easily be shortened with a pipe cutter at a bike shop.

Crankarms. Look on the back of the arms, and you'll see a number stamped in the metal. Arm lengths of 160 or 165 mm, rather than the standard 170 mm, are a better fit for women (and men) who have an inseam less than 29½ inches (measured from crotch to floor in bare feet). Keep in mind that mountain bike crankarms should be 5 mm longer than those on road bikes. The extra length gives you better leverage for steep climbs and slow-speed maneuvers. So the best size for your mountain bike will probably be 170 mm.

Saddle. Because women's pelvises are slightly wider than men's, the part of the pelvic bones they sit on (the ischial tuberosities) are farther apart. To support these bones and keep weight from resting solely on their genitalia, women generally need a saddle that's a little wider in the rear. You can usually find these anatomical saddles in stock at your local shop because sooner or later, many women want one in their quest for greater comfort.

Brake levers. With smaller hands and shorter fingers, many women can benefit from short-reach brake levers for their road bikes. Check at a shop for the models currently available. Usually, mountain bike levers don't need to be replaced because most have adjustment screws that let you shorten their distance to the bar.

Bikes for Women

With all of the component options to alter an off-the-rack bike, do you really need one that's designed specifically for women?

Most women who are tall and have long arms can do fine on a standard frame as long as the top tube is at the short end of the size range. Racers and triathletes striving for the most streamlined position are likely to prefer a bike that stretches them out more. You can adjust any bike to fit better as long as the standover height is correct (about 2 inches for a road bike; at least 3 inches for a mountain bike). You can get a shorter stem and wider saddle. You can move the seat forward a bit and tilt the handlebars up. You can install shorter crankarms and shorter-reach brake levers, or a taller stem that lets you sit more upright.

But trade-offs exist. A saddle shoved too far forward can cause inefficient pedaling and knee problems. A very short stem can result in squirrelly bike handling. If your bike setup is maxed out, you may not be able to make additional adjustments should your cycling style change. And for some women, all the adjustments in the world to a standard bike won't make their discomforts disappear.

Also, there are real advantages to getting a bike designed for women. For example, several major manufacturers offer models engineered specifically for the women most likely to have serious problems fitting on standard bikes—those under 5-foot-4. Bike models change every year, so check at shops to see what's currently available for women, even in brands you've looked at before.

Georgena Terry has built her women's cycling business by offering bikes to fit women from 4-foot-10 to 5-foot-11, not just those under 5-foot-4. No matter how tall a woman is, she notes, "her muscles are not only generally smaller than a man's but also distributed differently, resulting in more force on joints. A slightly more upright riding position eases those forces."

Not every woman needs a woman's bike. But every woman needs a bike that fits well, particularly in the critical distance between the seat and handlebar. A woman's bike may be the best place to start looking.

Clothing That Fits

If you're a new rider, you might wonder why women cyclists dress the way they do. Comfort and ease of movement are the big motivators.

Think about the sensitivity of the parts of your body that make contact with the bike—your hands, your feet, and your seat.

Until recently, cycling clothing for women would fit well only if you were built like a bicycle pump—or a man. Now, it's easier to find clothing sized for any woman's anatomy.

But don't trust all companies who claim to make women-specific clothing. Check the garments themselves instead of just the labels. For instance, anomalies such as overly large armholes on sleeveless jerseys suggest that a manufacturer is merely offering women a downsized version of a men's cut instead of a gender-specific design.

Otherwise, it's all out there—fabric prints ranging from feminine to ferocious; a take-your-pick palette of pastels, brights, earth tones, and basic black. Garments cut for road, off-road, or casual pedaling. Styles that say cycling, and others that look more like traditional clothing. Here are guidelines for buying several types of clothing and accessories.

Shorts, knickers, and tights. Putting thick-seamed shorts or blue jeans between you and the saddle will literally rub you the wrong way. You should wear cycling-specific shorts, knickers, or tights, which are designed to minimize bulk and prevent chafing.

The cling of spandex keeps shorts from riding up and exposing your thighs to chafing against the saddle. If you dislike the glossy racer look, you can find spandex blended with cotton or other materials. These reduce the shine but retain the form fit.

If the tight, second-skin look bothers you, go the camouflage route: made-for-cycling baggy shorts with built-in spandex shorts. These "baggies" have gained popularity for about-town cycling and trail use, although they're not going to be as comfortable as you'd like for long-distance road riding. And if you stand frequently as you ride, be forewarned that the outer short tends to catch on the nose of the saddle.

What's inside the garment counts, too. There should be a smooth, soft liner in the center that pads and protects you from friction. This liner is often called a chamois from the era when it was actually made of leather, but today's shorts use synthetic materials, which are more supple. Check the liner to make sure it doesn't have a seam running through the center because it can irritate tender tissues. Most women prefer a construction with two curved seams ("baseball stitching") that keep the center smooth. Even better is a molded, one-piece liner. Most shorts truly designed for women have one style or the other.

The under-the-liner padding may be fleece, gel, foam, or even liquid. Thicker may not mean better if the material bunches, so don't go by the amount of padding alone. Many liners have an antibacterial treatment, which helps reduce the chance of developing saddle sores. Lined cycling shorts are meant to be worn without underwear and washed after every use. Don't ride in unlined garments. If you have multisport tights, wear cycling shorts under them or try a thigh-length padded brief made for the purpose. Expect to pay from around $25 to $75 for a pair of cycling shorts. The same goes for long-legged cycling tights or knickers, which have legs that extend to just below the knee. The more expensive, the more individual panels (as many as eight) will be used in construction and, thus, the better the fit. Also, the liner and padding will be of higher quality. A good pair of shorts, properly cared for, can easily last for several seasons.

Gloves. For road and off-road riding, several manufacturers offer gloves cut to fit women's narrower hands and wrists. Expect to pay $15 to $30. Most are lightly padded for comfort. Gloves protect your hands from all sorts of wear and tear and improve your grip on the handlebar, so think of them more as a necessity rather than as an optional accessory.

Jerseys and crop tops. Cycling jerseys in women's proportions are available in more designs than ever. You can find virtually any cut, size, and neckline. Materials vary, but any good jersey will be made from a synthetic fabric that transports moisture away from your skin. Avoid cotton, which feels cold and clammy when damp.

Breezier crop tops come in short and to-the-waist lengths. The latter still provides air conditioning while reducing the wolf whistles. Some models have mesh panels for ventilation. Some come with a built-in bra. Whatever type of jersey you choose, it should have three rear pockets so you can easily carry snacks and other items. If you ride the road, choose colors that are bright enough to attract the eyes of motorists.

Jackets. A lightweight shell jacket that folds to slip into a jersey pocket or seatbag can save you from shivering if the air turns chilly or it begins to shower. Features to look for include zippered pockets for items you want handy, a front zipper that's easy to operate with one hand, comfortable elastic in the cuffs to keep sleeves where you want them, a tail long enough to cover you when you're bent toward the handlebar, and a color that makes you visible on a gray day. A shell should be made of breathable material or have vents so that you don't create your own rain shower inside.

Cover-ups. There may be times when you want to quickly put casual clothing over your cycling duds, like when you mix a ride with other activities and find yourself in a restaurant, store, party, or church. The solution is to carry a cotton wraparound skirt or pair of sweatpants in a bike bag. Some clothing companies make cover-ups that coordinate with their jerseys and shorts.

Shoes. Cycling shoes are necessary for serious riding because their rigid soles stop pedal pressure from hurting your feet. Shoes are designed for road riding or mountain biking, with the latter type offering the advantage of easier walking—the cleat for clipless pedals is recessed into the sole. Unfortunately, shoe selection is limited in the smallest women's sizes. You may have to try unisex sizing, which does accommodate many women.

Helmets. Good fit in a helmet means that it stays securely in place when you're riding over bumps and, most important, if you crash. To help this happen, many newer helmets feature a "locking system" against the rear of the head. This extra strap customizes the fit and keeps the helmet from bouncing or moving too far forward or backward. With such a system, unisex helmets will probably fit most women. But ponytails can interfere with the locking system in some models, so if you tie back your hair for cycling, check before you buy. A few companies make helmets specifically for women, and ponytail clearance is not a problem with these.

4
Road Riding Position

To ride your best, it's essential that your bike fits you as perfectly as possible. The key is to adjust your bike to accommodate your body rather than to force your body to conform to the bike. Use the following setup advice and riding tips to arrive at the most comfortable and efficient position.

1. Arms. Beware road rider's rigor mortis. Keep your elbows bent and relaxed to absorb shock and to prevent veering when you hit a bump. Keep arms in line with your body, not splayed to the side, to make a more compact, aerodynamic package.

2. Upper body/shoulders. The operative words: Be still. Imagine the calories burned by rocking side to side with every pedal stroke on a 25-mile ride. Use that energy for pedaling. Also, beware of creeping forward on the saddle and hunching your back when tired. Shift to a higher gear and stand to pedal periodically to prevent stiffness in your hips and back.

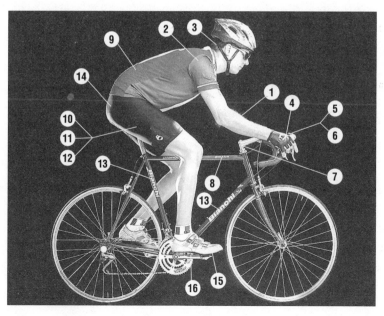

3. Head and neck. Avoid putting your head down, especially when you're tired. Periodically tilt your head side to side to stretch and relax neck muscles.

4. Hands. Change hand position frequently to prevent finger numbness and upper-body stiffness. A white-knuckle hold on the handlebar is unnecessary and will produce energy-sapping muscle tension throughout the arms and shoulders. Grasp the drops for descents or high-speed riding, and the brake lever hoods for relaxed cruising. On long climbs, hold the top of the bar to sit upright and open the chest for easier breathing. When standing, grasp the hoods lightly and gently rock the bike side to side in sync with your pedal strokes. Always keep each thumb and a finger closed around the hood or bar to prevent losing hold on an unexpected bump.

5. Handlebar. Bar width should equal shoulder width. Err on the side of a wider one to open your chest for breathing. Some models are available with a large drop (vertical distance) to help big hands fit into the hooks. Position the flat, bottom portion of the bar horizontal or pointed slightly down toward the rear brake.

6. Brake levers. Levers can be moved around the curve of the bar to give you the best compromise between holding the hoods and braking when your hands are in the bar hooks. Most riders do best if the lever tips touch a straightedge extended forward from under the flat, bottom portion of the bar.

7. Stem height. With the stem high enough (normally about an inch below the top of the saddle), you'll be more inclined to use the drops. Putting it lower can improve aerodynamics but may be uncomfortable. Never position the stem above its maximum extension line, or your weight on the bar could cause it to break.

8. Top-tube and stem length. These combined dimensions, which determine your reach, vary according to your flexibility and anatomy. There is no ultimate prescription, but there is a good starting point: When you're comfortably seated with elbows slightly bent and hands on the brake hoods, the front hub should be obscured by the handlebar. This is a relatively upright position, and with time, you may benefit from a longer stem extension to improve aerodynamics and flatten your back.

9. Back. A flat back is the defining mark of a well-positioned rider. The correct stem and top-tube combination is crucial for this, but so is hip flexibility. Concentrate on rotating the top of your hips forward. If you think of trying to touch the top tube with your stomach, it will help stop you from rounding your back.

10. Saddle height. There are various formulas for this, but you needn't be a mathematician to know what the correct height looks like. Your knees should be slightly bent at the bottom of the pedal stroke and your hips shouldn't rock on the saddle (when viewed from behind). Try this quick method, which is used at the Olympic Training Center in Colorado Springs, Colorado.

Set the height so that there is 5 mm of clearance between your heel and the pedal at the bottom of the stroke. Add a few millimeters if your shoes have very thin soles at the heel compared to the forefoot. Also, raise the saddle 2 or 3 mm if you have long feet in proportion to your height. For those who have knee pain caused by chondromalacia, a saddle on the higher side of the acceptable range can be therapeutic, so gradually raise it until hip rocking begins, then lower it slightly. Make saddle height changes 2 mm at a time to avoid leg strain.

11. Saddle tilt. The saddle should be level, which you can check by laying a yardstick along its length. A slight downward tilt may be more comfortable if you're using an extreme forward position with an aero bar and elbow rests, but too much causes you to slide forward and place excessive weight on your arms.

12. Fore/aft saddle position. The trend is to move the saddle back to produce more power for climbing. To start with, sit comfortably in the center of the saddle with the crankarms horizontal. Drop a plumb line from the front of your forward kneecap. It should touch the end of the crankarm. This is the neutral position, and you should be able to achieve it by loosening the seatpost clamp and sliding the saddle fore or aft. Climbers, time trialists, and some road racers prefer the line to fall a couple of centimeters behind the end of the crankarm to increase leverage in big gears. Conversely, track and criterium racers like a more forward position to improve leg speed. Remember, if your reach to the handlebar is wrong, use stem length to correct it, not fore/aft saddle position.

13. Frame. With your bare feet 6 inches apart, measure your inseam from crotch to floor, then multiply by 0.65. This equals your road frame size, measured along the seat tube from the center of the crank axle to the center of the top tube. As a double check, this should produce 4 to 5 inches of exposed seatpost when your saddle height is correct. (The post's maximum-extension line shouldn't show, of course.)

14. Buttocks. By sliding rearward or forward on the saddle, you can emphasize different muscle groups. This can be useful on a long climb. Moving forward emphasizes the quadriceps muscle on the front of your thigh, while moving back accentuates the hamstrings and glutes on the back.

15. Feet. Look at your footprints as you walk from a swimming pool. Some of us are pigeon-toed and others are duck-footed. To prevent knee injury, strive for a cleat position that accommodates your natural foot angle. Make cleat adjustments on rides until you feel right, or pay a shop to do it using a fitting device. Better still, use a clipless pedal system that allows your feet to pivot freely, or float, thus making precise adjustment unnecessary. Position cleats fore/aft so the widest part of each foot is directly above or slightly in front of the pedal axle.

16. Crankarm length. The trend is toward longer levers. These add power but may inhibit pedaling speed. In general, if your inseam is less than 29 inches, use 165-mm crankarms; 29 to 32 inches, 170 mm; 33 to 34 inches, 172.5 mm; and more than 34 inches, 175 mm. Crankarm length is measured from the center of the fixing bolt to the center of the pedal mounting hole. It's usually stamped on the back of the arm.

5
Mountain Biking Position

Off-road riding is full of variations—your position on the bike is always changing as you pedal over undulating terrain. Even so, there are several important setup dimensions and riding techniques that will help you perform better. Spend a few minutes going through these guidelines, then go have a great ride.

1. Frame. Spontaneous (sometimes unwanted) dismounts are a part of riding off-road. Consequently, you need lots of clearance between you and the top tube. The ideal mountain bike size is 3 to 4 inches smaller than your road bike size. This isn't as critical if you'll be riding only on pavement or smooth dirt roads, but there's no advantage to having a frame any larger than the smallest size that provides enough saddle height and reach to the handlebar. Smaller frames are lighter, stiffer, and more maneuverable. Because manufacturers specify frame size in different ways, use the stand-over test. When straddling the bike while wearing your riding shoes, there should be 3 inches or more between your crotch and the top tube.

2. Saddle height. Seatpost lengths of 350 mm are common, so a lot of post can be out of the frame before the maximum-extension line shows. For efficient pedaling, your knee should remain slightly bent at the bottom of the pedal stroke (the same as with a road bike). You may wish to lower the saddle slightly for rough terrain, enabling you to rise up so the bike can float beneath you without pounding your crotch. On steep descents, some riders drop the saddle even farther to keep their weight low and rearward, but others just slide their buttocks off the back.

3. Saddle tilt. Most off-road riders prefer a level saddle, but some (including many women) find a slight nose-down tilt avoids pressure and irritation. Others go slightly nose up, which helps them sit back and lessen strain on their arms.

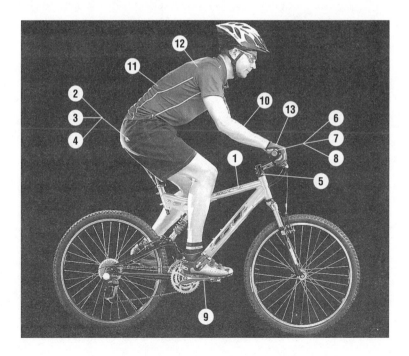

4. Fore/aft saddle position. This variable is not for adjusting your reach to the handlebar—that's why stems come with different extensions. Use the same procedure described for roadies on page 21.

5. Stem. Mountain bike stems come in a huge variety of extensions (from 60 to 150 mm) and rises (from −5 to +25 degrees). For good control, the stem should place the bar an inch or two below the top of the saddle. This helps put weight on the front wheel so it's easier to steer on climbs and less likely to leave the ground. Never exceed the stem's maximum-height line, or it could break and cause a nasty crash. The extension should allow comfortably bent arms and a straight back. A longer and lower reach works for fast cruising, but a higher, closer hand position affords more control on difficult trails.

6. Handlebar width. An end-to-end measurement of 21 to 24 inches is common. If the bar seems too wide, it can be trimmed with a hacksaw or pipe cutter. First, though, move your controls and grips inward and take a ride to make sure you'll like the new width. And remember to leave a bit extra at each end if you use bar-ends. In general, the narrower the handlebar, the quicker the steering. Wider bars provide more control at slow speed.

7. Handlebar sweep. Flat bars can be straight or have up to 11 degrees of rearward bend per side. The choice is strictly one of arm and wrist comfort. Be aware that changing the sweep also changes your reach to the grips and could require a different stem length. Bars with an upward bend or rise are also available. These can allow a lower stem position.

8. Bar-ends. These short, forward extensions are great for climbing leverage and achieving a longer, lower position on flat fire roads or pavement. Angle them slightly upward. Models that curve inward help protect the hands and are less likely to snag brush on tight singletrack. If you're thinking of installing bar-ends, make sure your handlebar can accept them. Some ultralight bars can't.

9. Crankarm length. Manufacturers usually vary this with frame size. For greater leverage on steep climbs, mountain bikes typically come with crankarms 5 mm longer than would a road bike for the same size rider.

10. Arms. Slightly bent arms act as shock absorbers. If you can reach the bar only with straight elbows, get a shorter stem or condition yourself to lean forward more by rotating your hips.

Tips for Hybrid Riders

Hybrids (also known as cross bikes) generally have 700C wheels like a road bike but a flat handlebar like a mountain bike. They are close to road bikes for most dimensions. If you'll be riding it off-road, you may wish to select a frame size at the small end of your acceptable range for greater crotch clearance. Some hybrids also have a higher bottom bracket than road bikes, which means their stand-over height will be less for the identical size frame. Strive for at least 2 inches of clearance between your crotch and the top tube.

Many hybrids also come with a short, high-rise stem, which supplies an upright position for casual riding. In time, you may wish to install a longer stem with less rise. It will get you closer to a 45-degree back angle, which is ideal for mountain biking.

11. Back. When your top-tube/stem-length combo is correct, you should have a forward lean of about 45 degrees during normal riding. This is an efficient angle because the strong gluteus muscles of the buttocks don't contribute much to pedaling when you're sitting more upright. Plus, a forward lean shifts some weight to the arms, so your butt doesn't get as sore.

12. Upper body. Don't hunch your shoulders, and you'll avoid muscle soreness and fatigue. Tilt your head every few minutes to stave off tight neck muscles.

13. Hands and wrists. Grasp the bar just firmly enough to maintain control. Set the brake levers close to the grips and angle them so that you can extend a finger or two around each and still hold the bar comfortably. Your wrists should be straight when you're standing over the saddle and braking, as on a downhill. Always ride with your thumbs under the bar so that your hands can't slip off.

6

Safety First on the Road

It may sound crazy, but cyclists should try to make life easier for motorists. After all, it's in our self-interest to make the road a safer, more pleasant place. Here are 10 easy ways to minimize the chance of conflict. These are particularly effective for new or casual cyclists who have yet to develop the necessary confidence, fitness, or bike-handling ability to be assertive in traffic.

1. Ride with traffic. Pedestrians are taught to walk on the left side of the road, against the flow of traffic. Many new cyclists assume that they should do the same. This is wrong for several reasons. First, a bicycle is recognized as a vehicle in all 50 states, which means cyclists are lawfully bound to ride just as if they were driving a car or a motorcycle. Cyclists have all the rights of motorists and all of the same responsibilities.

Second, it's much safer to ride with traffic. You become part of the normal flow of vehicles, so drivers won't be surprised by your appearance in unexpected places. Otherwise, you'll be in danger of cars pulling out or turning in front of you. Finally, if a car is going 40 mph and you're pedaling toward it at 15 mph, you're approaching each other at 55 mph. But if you're traveling in the same direction, the car overtakes you at only 25 mph and the driver has more time to respond.

2. Keep right. Barring potholes, storm grates, parked cars, glass, and other hazards, it's usually easier and safer to ride to the right. If there is no safe shoulder, however, ride as far to the left of the white road-edge line as it takes to prevent drivers from attempting to squeeze past and put you in danger. Just avoid being in the traffic flow for no apparent reason.

3. Use common sense about riding abreast. It's enjoyable to ride side by side with a companion and carry on a conversation. But road and traffic conditions may be such that vehicles back up behind you when they could otherwise get by. So restrict your side-by-side riding to quiet, secondary roads. Even if you're alone, traffic may back up, especially on narrow, winding roads with limited visibility. Wave vehicles by when the path is clear.

4. Don't force vehicles to repass you needlessly. Let's say you're riding along a narrow, busy road and motorists are having trouble getting by. There are a half-dozen waiting at the next red light, all of whom have already patiently overtaken you. Do you maintain your place in line, or do you zip past everyone on the right so that you'll get the jump when the light changes? If you do the latter, you might gain 50 feet and save a few seconds, but you're also likely to create six drivers who are annoyed at you and cyclists in general because they're caught behind you again.

Admittedly, the scenario becomes trickier if, by hanging back, you miss the light. There are two tactful ways around this: One is to move up in line only far enough to make it through the light. The other is to ride to the light, but move out slowly and slightly to the right when it turns green, letting the cars through the intersection first. One other courtesy at traffic lights: Avoid blocking drivers who want to turn right on red.

5. Ride predictably. Ride in a straight line when you're cruising, and use hand signals when turning or changing lanes. Hand signals are a courtesy and an important part of safe cycling. Point with your left arm for a left turn, and your right arm for a right turn. Hold your left arm down with palm facing rearward to indicate a stop. Motorists feel more comfortable dealing with cyclists who communicate their intentions. More important, drivers tend to show them more respect.

If you're riding erratically, it's difficult for drivers to know when to pass. They may let several relatively safe opportunities go by before becoming exasperated and taking a dangerous chance. Don't zip in and out of traffic, run stop signs, hop curbs, or try to outsprint drivers. Think of the things that irritate you most about cyclists when you're driving, and don't do them.

6. Avoid busy roads. It's surprising how often you see cyclists on a busy highway, ruffling the delicate feathers of already edgy commuters. An alternate route doesn't have to be a residential street with stop signs every other block or a glass-littered, jogger-strewn bike path. Examine a map of your area, and you'll probably be surprised at the selection of relatively quiet secondary roads that can help you escape traffic.

7. Make yourself visible. In conditions where motorists might not readily see you (an overcast day, for example), it's a courtesy and plain good sense to wear brightly colored clothes. Drivers will never blame themselves when they almost pull into your path after a too-casual glance. Yes, it's unfair. But you can greatly enhance your safety by dressing in red, orange, yellow, or other flashy hues. At night, it's a different story. Drivers who encounter cyclists riding without lights, reflectors, and light-colored clothes are right to consider them menaces.

8. Ride defensively. Stay alert and anticipate the actions of motorists. Lift your nose off the handlebar and analyze traffic situations, just as you do when driving. One trick is to look drivers directly in the eye at intersections. This will tell you if they're daydreaming or if they know you're there. How can you tell if a car is about to pull out? Watching the front wheels is the surest way to spot movement.

Use your ears as well as your eyes. Listen for vehicles overtaking you. With practice, you'll even be able to gauge how close they might come. Never wear personal-stereo headphones because they deprive you of this valuable protection. In fact, they're illegal for cycling in most states.

9. Be careful about "provocative" actions. At a red light, even friendly drivers are likely to be irritated by a cyclist riding in circles in front of them. Similarly, if you lean on a vehicle at a stoplight, be aware that some drivers consider their cars extensions of themselves. You wouldn't want anyone leaning on your bike, would you?

Should a motorist cut you off or yell something at you, resist the urge to make an obscene gesture or shout profanities. Remember, you're dealing with a machine that can kill or maim you, and a driver who may even be carrying a weapon. The best reaction is no reaction unless you are purposely being harassed. If so, get the license number and best description you can, and call the police from the next phone you see.

10. Return the favor. Cyclists appreciate little unexpected courtesies from motorists. You nod a thank-you to the driver who has the right-of-way but waves you through anyway. Try returning the favor. You might, for example, motion a driver to make his turn in front of you if you'll be slow getting under way. Who knows? That driver might look a bit more favorably on the next cyclist down the road.

PART TWO

Skills and Techniques

7
Your First Riding Lesson

It's time to stop reading about cycling and start doing it. So get on your bike and go for a quick introductory spin. You'll discover how to shift gears, ride a straight line, corner, climb, and descend. Soon, you'll be riding like a pro.

First, loosen up a bit. Lots of riders don't stretch because it's easy to warm up simply by pedaling for a few minutes. That's a good idea anyway, but stretching is better insurance against muscle strains.

To loosen your back muscles, gently turn your torso back and forth while standing with your arms extended to the side and legs apart. To stretch the muscles in the front of your thighs (quadriceps), stand on your left leg, bend the right knee back, and reach behind to grasp your foot with your left hand. Slowly pull your foot toward your buttocks, then repeat for the other leg. To loosen the muscles in the back of your thighs (hamstrings), sit on the ground with one leg extended and the other bent so that the sole of your foot rests against the inside of your thigh. Then reach toward the toes of your extended leg. Repeat for the other leg.

Remember, stretching should be done with smooth, gentle movements. Hold each stretch for 20 to 30 seconds so the muscles have the opportunity to relax in the extended position. If it starts to hurt, stop.

Shifting

For your first few rides, it's best to stick to bike paths and the bike lanes marked on the side of the road. There's no sense riding in traffic until you feel comfortable. Your confidence will increase quickly if you spend the first few rides concentrating on riding skills rather than watching for cars. Pedal easily in low-resistance gears for 10 minutes to further loosen your legs. (Do the same at the end of the ride to cool down. Postride stretching helps, too.)

As you spin along, shift a few times to familiarize yourself with your bike's gear system. The left shift lever controls the front derailleur and moves the chain between chainrings. Feel how much less resistance there is when the chain is on the smallest ring. This is where you want it to be when you are going up a hill or riding into a strong headwind.

The right shift lever controls the rear derailleur and moves the chain among the cassette cogs. Feel how the pedaling resistance decreases as the chain goes from the smallest to the largest cog and increases as it moves in the opposite direction. By shifting to the appropriate gear (larger cogs for climbing, smaller cogs for descending and fast flatland riding), you'll be able to maintain a comfortable pedaling rate, or cadence, and conserve energy. The idea is to choose a gear combination that lets you keep a cadence of about 90 rpm in most conditions. You can calculate cadence by counting the number of times your right leg reaches the bottom of its pedal stroke in 30 seconds, then multiplying by two. The correct gear is any gear that lets you spin the pedals at this rate.

Riding a Straight Line

Riding a straight line is not as simple as it sounds. Weaving is dangerous. It annoys fellow riders and could turn you into a motorist's hood ornament. Cycling coach Roger Young of Corona del Mar, California, suggests looking no closer than 20 feet ahead when riding at 10 to 15 mph. Add a foot or so for every additional mile per hour. You'll be a lot less steady if you look right in front of your wheel. Keep your wrists and elbows relaxed. Steer with your hips, not just your arms. Try twisting your hips on the saddle, and you'll get the idea. Stay loose and balanced, spin smoothly instead of stabbing at the pedals, and look ahead at the line (imaginary or not) that you want the bike to follow.

Pedaling is an art—you can spot good riders by how they seem to flow along. Their knees are aligned with the bike, not splayed outward. They don't pedal, coast, pedal, coast. Instead, they keep the pedals turning and press a little harder or a little softer to smoothly control their speed. This comes with practice, so think about your technique every time you ride. Remember to pull the pedals up rather than just push down. You don't have to pull hard, but by reducing the weight of each leg during the upward part of the stroke, you'll help the opposite leg apply more power. To get the knack, imagine you're scraping mud off the sole of your shoe each time it comes through the bottom of the stroke. This will help your transition from pushing down to pulling up.

Turning

Before beginning a turn, check for anything coming up from behind. If it's clear, move a bit in the opposite direction of the turn for a better angle through the turn. Stop pedaling with the inside pedal up, then lean your bike into the turn, and coast through. For added stability and increased traction, try scooting toward the back of the saddle. Press harder on the outside pedal, too. The more weight you put on it, the more steeply you can lean the bike. Once you start turning, don't brake or make any major change in your line or you could lose control.

The principle is the same for turns in either direction. To improve quickly, practice turning in quiet residential streets, an industrial park after hours, or in a big empty parking lot.

Climbing

Climbing really isn't that difficult, though plenty of riders dread hills more than any other challenge in cycling. The trick to cutting climbs down to size is being smart with your gear system.

Get into a lower gear just as the hill starts. If the chain isn't on the smallest chainring, shift there. It's where you need to be for the bike's lowest (easiest to pedal) gears. If you wait until you are already pushing hard on the climb, the chain won't shift as well, or it might not shift at all. If you start to strain and still need a lower gear, shift to a larger rear cog. As you do, lighten your pedal pressure for one revolution so the chain can move smoothly, then resume pushing.

Climbing style is a matter of preference. Some riders like to stay seated on long climbs, pedaling a low gear fairly quickly. Road bike riders will have their hands well-spaced on top of the handlebar (not down on the drops) so they're sitting upright and can breathe easier. An aerodynamic position isn't needed when going uphill. Let your upper body bob rhythmically in synch with your pedal strokes.

Other riders prefer to do most of their climbing out of the saddle. They put their hands on the brake lever hoods (or bar-ends of a mountain bike), stand up, and let the bike rock side to side beneath them. In this way, they can apply their body weight to each downward pedal stroke. Experiment with both styles to find the one that works better for you. Chances are good that you'll want to use both, depending on a hill's length and steepness.

A large part of climbing is psychological. To avoid becoming demoralized, focus on the road in front of you rather than that distant summit. Have confidence that you can make it to the top. You can, if you are in the right gear and don't go so hard that you run out of breath or set your muscles on fire. One trick used even by racers is to start going up in a lower gear than you actually need. This ensures that you won't blow up, and if you're feeling good, you can even shift to a higher gear near the top to go faster. View hills as a challenge that will make you stronger, because they will.

Descending

Getting down the hill is the fun part. As your speed increases over the top of the climb, shift progressively to smaller cogs and then to the biggest chainring. If the hill is long and steep enough you'll wind up in the smallest cog (high gear). Then, instead of coasting, keep pedaling to retain your bike's stability and keep your legs loose. If your bike starts to shimmy, stop pedaling and squeeze its top tube between your knees. Don't keep the brakes on all the time, or your rims could overheat and cause a blowout. Instead, alternately pump the front and rear brake to control your speed.

To handle a corner when descending, brake to a safe speed, pick your line, and take it as you did before—butt back, inside pedal up, weight on the outside pedal, and brakes released.

8
Road Skills

As you get into cycling, you're bound to have at least one riding partner who drives you crazy. He doesn't ride any more than you do. His bike isn't any lighter. He doesn't take steroids (probably). And yet you just can't keep up with him. He drops you on climbs, descents, corners . . . you name it. You're going nuts trying to figure out why.

The answer is easy. He has a few skills that you're lacking. You could kneel at the cleats of some cycling Zen master for years, learning the secrets of this seemingly simple sport (which is actually pretty rich and complex). Or you could take just a few minutes to study the details outlined in this chapter.

Cornering

The right technique will make turns easier and safer even as you take them faster.

1. Put your hands on the drops, using a relaxed grip.

2. Spread your weight so that you can steer from the rear of the saddle.

3. Keep the inside pedal up.

4. Straighten the outside leg and put your weight on that pedal.

5. Look ahead at the line you want the bike to follow.

6. Brake before the turn, then stay off the brakes during the turn.

7. If traffic allows, approach the turn by starting wide, then cut to its apex, and exit wide.

8. Lean your bike more than your body as you round the turn.

Accelerating

A well-timed jump is often enough to surprise and beat stronger riders—or quick stoplights.

1. Select the gear you want, put your hands on the drops, and bend your elbows.

2. Spring smoothly out of the saddle, moving up and forward.

3. Simultaneously, apply full power to your dominant-side crankarm (usually the right one if you're right-handed), when it's at about the 2 o'clock position.

4. At the same time, pull on the handlebar to counterbalance your leg thrust. Keep your head and shoulders steady.

5. Gradually move your weight farther forward as you accelerate.

6. Shift to the next higher gear (smaller cog) if you begin to spin out.

Looking Back

To ride safely in traffic, sometimes you need eyes in the back of your head. You could use a rearview mirror, or you could learn to quickly glance over your shoulder without swerving.

1. Stay seated and keep pedaling.

2. For stability and a more upright position, grasp the brake lever hoods.

3. Relax your upper body and bend your elbows.

4. Turn your head to the left without twisting your shoulders or hips.

5. Glance back out of the corner of your eye for just a second, then return your attention to the road ahead.

Drafting

Many riders stay too far behind their partner's rear wheel for fear of hitting it and crashing. The key to getting a good-yet-safe draft is staying within 12 inches and constantly making subtle speed adjustments to match your friend's pace.

1. Place your hands on the brake lever hoods or in the hooks of the handlebar so that you can quickly reach the brakes in an emergency, but try not to use them to control your speed.

2. Watch your partner's whole bike and body, not just his rear wheel, so you can anticipate his next move. Be attentive but relaxed.

3. Frequently look over or around your partner to see what's ahead.

4. If your front wheel gets closer than 6 inches, soft-pedal for a few strokes, but don't coast.

5. If you're still too close, move a few inches to the left—without overlapping wheels—so more wind catches you and slows you.

Seated Climbing

Instead of trying to alternately lift and stomp the pedals, concentrate on pushing each one forward, then pulling it back. This will smooth your stroke and allow you to apply force more evenly and efficiently.

1. As your right crankarm approaches 11 o'clock, apply force to the pedal as if you were pushing it forward and down. Visualize walking down long, shallow stairs.

2. Continue this pressure until the crankarm reaches 5 o'clock.

3. Now start clawing back and up on the pedal as if you were scraping something from the bottom of your shoe.

4. Continue this until the crankarm again approaches 11 o'clock, then repeat the process.

5. Use the same technique with the left leg.

Out-of-Saddle Climbing

The key is getting your torso to work in sync with your legs. Too much upper-body force wastes energy and makes you weave dangerously. If you don't use enough force, you might as well be sitting.

1. Rest the crotch of your hands on the brake lever hoods, not on the drops where control is worse and deep breathing is more difficult.

2. As you push down on the left pedal, pull easily up on the bar with your left hand. Don't grip it too tightly.

3. Let the bike rock to the right, but no more than a foot at the bar.

4. Do the reverse as you push the right pedal, letting the bike rock to the left.

5. Use your body weight to help drive the pedals downward.

Going Fast on the Flats

To go fast, you have to be aerodynamic. Many riders think this means learning to endure discomfort, but here's a way to get low and stay comfortable.

1. Put your hands on the drops.

2. Slide your buttocks to the rear of the saddle.

3. Bend forward at the hips as if your midsection were hinged. The goal is to make your back flat, not humped. Envision trying to touch the top tube with your belly button.

4. Bend your elbows so that your forearms are almost parallel to the top tube.

5. Rather than lowering your head at the neck, drop your shoulders.

Descending

It's easy to go fast downhill—just let 'er rip. And it's easy to be safe—just keeping squeezing the brakes. But it's better to do some of each.

1. Put your hands on the drops so you're in an aero position but can still reach the brake levers.

2. Soft-pedal to keep your muscles from getting stiff. Be in a high gear so you can accelerate out of corners or through flatter parts of the descent.

3. When you descend, your weight shifts forward, which undercuts stability. Slide back on the saddle to rebalance your weight.

4. Drop your torso to keep your center of gravity low.

5. Feather both brakes simultaneously or alternately to moderate speed. To avoid overheating the rims, don't apply either for more than a few seconds at a time.

6. To reduce speed by several miles per hour, sit up to catch air rather than braking.

7. Look 40 to 50 feet down the road at the line you want the bike to take.

9
Off-Road Skills

Like all of the best things in life, mountain biking seduces you and scares the heck out of you at the same time. Surfing trails and dirt roads on fat, knobby tires brings out the kid in all of us but without that immediate and effortless ease that kids use to master new sports. Mountain biking can be the ultimate joyride, but it can also be quite discouraging for beginners.

Fortunately, anyone can learn to roll over logs, finesse a path through rocks, descend steep pitches, and handle other off-road obstacles. It's never as hard as it seems. Here's a guide to some of the most valuable basic mountain biking skills. They range from intangible concepts to step-by-step techniques and they'll all make you a better mountain biker.

Just Relax

The chief physical demand of mountain biking resembles the lifestyles of the sport's best riders: hang loose. Almost all beginners stiffen when they get on a trail. If you ride with your limbs locked, your bike won't be able to flow. Instead of rising over a rock, your front wheel will stick when you hit. A single errant jerk of your arm will pull the bike off balance.

To make sure you're riding loose, check your elbows, knees, hands, and even your jaw muscles. These body parts are barometers—if they're not tight, the rest of your body won't be.

Forget About the Small Stuff

One of the biggest mistakes new off-road riders make is trying to avoid everything. They react to every pebble and twig in their paths. Mountain bikes are designed to ride over most obstacles without tipping or slipping.

In time, you'll learn what deserves your attention. Until then, use this technique to help yourself develop good judgment: For each section, concentrate on only a single aspect of riding the trail. This might be trying to stay on a narrow edge. Or it might be rolling over rocks or staying out of a rut.

Another way to practice focusing is to pick a "peak" move from the next 10 feet of trail. Select a challenge that will require the most skill—a big rock, a tough log, a tight turn—and concentrate on getting through that. The small stuff will happen automatically.

Learn How to See

Your eyes must develop off-road vision. One thing this means is that you must train yourself not to look at obstacles you want to avoid. Instead, look at the path, or line, that you want to take—where you want to go instead of what you want to miss. This is important because your steering follows your vision. If you look at a jagged rock that's narrowing the trail, you'll ride into it. Focus on the gap that will take you safely past the rock.

Off-road vision also involves learning how far you should look ahead. In the slowest, toughest sections, you might eye only the next 6 feet of trail. On a fast, smooth, dirt-road descent, you might look 20 to 30 feet ahead. Most beginners mistakenly cast their gaze too short—just in front of the wheel. This causes your riding to be purely reactionary. All you're doing is responding to the trail from moment to moment— you can't plan, anticipate, and see the good line.

Assume the Position

There's a basic stance that readies your body for changing conditions. Former world champion Ned Overend calls it the attack position. You should ride in it as often as possible. You'll alter it slightly to give yourself more control for downhilling, climbing, turning, and other moves.

Keep both legs bent equally, crankarms parallel to the ground. Your buttocks should not be planted on the saddle. They should lightly graze the surface, able to move around. Your elbows should be well-bent, and your head should be up. You're like a cat, ready to pounce.

In this position, you can easily make the weight shifts and other body movements that will help you roll over things, hop the bike, stay upright and in control on downhills, and perform other maneuvers. In addition, this position lets you absorb shocks and jolts with bent knees and elbows.

Roll Over Obstacles

The following tips work well for rocks, roots, and bumps no taller than 6 inches.

Make sure you have enough speed. This keeps your bike from stopping when you hit the obstacle, helps prevent the front wheel from twisting sideways on impact, and is vital to getting the entire bike over. Most newcomers are reluctant to ride very fast when they're approaching something, so here's the trick: Have enough speed so that even if you don't pedal for 2 feet before the impact, you'll have enough momentum to roll over the object.

Lighten up. Just before your front wheel contacts the obstacle, lighten, or unweight it, by shifting your body slightly rearward and pulling back on the handlebar. Keep your elbows loose, but grip the bar firmly enough to prevent it from twisting when the wheel hits.

Absorb the impact with your flexed knees and elbows. When the front wheel hits, let the bike come up toward your chest. Your elbows should bend as this happens.

Reach out. When your front wheel hits the ground on the other side, extend your arms. This pushes the bike away from you (forward) and helps bring the rear wheel over.

Keep moving. Unweight the rear wheel by shifting your weight forward. Otherwise, it will pop off the obstacle and shoot you over the bar or catch on the obstacle and stop you dead.

For bigger obstacles, you need to do a wheelie—actually pull the front wheel off the ground. This is mainly accomplished with a more exaggerated unweighting. Also, just as you lift the front, give one hard pedal stroke. This helps raise the wheel.

Climb with Power

Seated climbing saves energy and gives you more control and traction in most situations. Here are some techniques to scale the slopes.

Pick the right gear. Shift into a gear that lets you spin freely but without flailing. Slow, hard pedal revolutions aren't efficient and can cause you to lose traction or stall out.

Center your weight. As the pitch steepens, slightly scoot your butt back on the saddle, and put your nose closer to the handlebar. This keeps your weight centered between the wheels. If it's too close to the handlebar, your rear tire will slip. But if it's too far away, your front wheel will rise off the ground. You'll need to experiment to find the right position because every climb is different.

Keep pedaling. Many newcomers bail as soon as they feel one of the wheels begin to lose traction. If you keep your feet moving, you can adjust your weight to find the spot that regains traction. Hang with it.

Act like a sailor. For really steep stuff, bring your body forward until the nose of the saddle is between the cheeks of your butt, and your nose is close to the bar. With each pedal thrust, pull back on the bar with both hands. In this unorthodox (but effective) position, you can "row" your way up almost anything.

Some mountain bikers prefer to climb out of the saddle. This is most effective on bumpy, technical uphills when you need to move the bike

Obey the Rules

Trail access is a privilege for mountain bikers, not a guaranteed right. As a new rider, you must do your part to help keep trails open to all cyclists by obeying the International Mountain Bicycling Association's (IMBA) "Rules of the Trail."

■ Ride on open trails only.

■ Leave no trace.

■ Control your bicycle.

■ Always yield trail to pedestrians and equestrians.

■ Never scare animals.

■ Plan ahead.

underneath you or pull it over obstacles while climbing. It's also good for giving your muscles a break on extended ascents.

Just before you stand, move your hands toward the ends of your handlebar or onto the bar-ends if your bike has them. Shift into a harder gear (smaller cog) as you stand. If the front wheel rises, move your body slightly forward. If the rear wheel spins, move back. The trick is to find and keep the perfect weight distribution all the way to the top.

Descend with Confidence

Controlled descending depends on two factors: good braking and keeping your weight back.

Use both brakes. Most beginners, afraid of getting pitched over the handlebar, use too much rear brake and not enough front. This causes out-of-control skidding. It's important to use both. The front brake is more powerful, but it's not what causes faceplants (a wreck in which the rider goes over the bar and lands on his mug).

Shift your weight back. As you brake, you must distribute more of your weight to the rear. This keeps the bike from tipping forward. At first, you can keep the rear wheel on the ground simply by scooting your butt to the back of the saddle. Straighten your arms as you do this, but remember to keep your elbows loose, not locked.

As the descent steepens, you might need to push your butt completely off the saddle. In this extreme position, with the seat under your stomach, you can safely descend scary-steep downhills.

Don't brake so hard that the wheels stop moving. It's especially important to keep the front wheel spinning. You'll have more control.

10
Nine Common Mistakes to Avoid

Cycling is a deceptively simple sport. You hop on the saddle, push the pedals, and voilà, you're a cyclist, right? Well, yes and no.

Sure, bike riders don't have to memorize plays as in football or remember to hit the cutoff man as in baseball or figure out soccer's offsides rule. But you can still make mistakes that spoil your fun and retard your improvement. Here are nine common things that new cyclists do wrong—along with guidelines on how to do them right.

1. Always riding alone. You'll learn faster with a good teacher, so ask experienced riders if you can join them on their easy days. Watch how they corner or climb. Don't be afraid to ask for advice. Most good riders are happy to share information. Do a club ride and try to hang with the lead group for 5 miles. Next week, shoot for 10.

On singletrack, follow adept descenders and emulate the line they choose. Notice when they shift and brake, how they clear obstacles, and what extreme terrains they can ride. Look for a mentor. Good riders will make effortless moves that you hadn't dreamed of trying on your own. Following them extends the limits of what is possible.

2. Not eating or drinking. Have you ever stopped for chow at a scenic spot, then noticed how much stronger and faster you rode shortly thereafter? Food is fuel, so keep your tank full. On road rides, perfect your ability to unwrap an energy bar or peel a banana on the roll. And a midride picnic is an honorable mountain biking tradition.

Fluids are important, too. Adequate hydration increases the distance you can ride. It lowers perceived effort and allows you to recover faster. Don't leave home without at least one big bottle of water or sports drink. Take two bottles if you're mountain biking. You can significantly improve your endurance with no additional training simply by packing in the fluid.

3. Never resting. Rest is as important as training. As you relax after hard efforts, recuperation, growth, and improvement take place. Think of it this way: If you're still tired from Sunday's tough ride, you're still recovering and improving. According to Ed Burke, Ph.D., cycling physiologist and director of the exercise-science program at the University of Colorado at Colorado Springs, "It takes up to 48 hours after you've exercised to exhaustion to replenish the muscles' glycogen stores." Don't short-circuit this refueling process by forcing yourself to ride hard again too soon. The ability to make yourself rest when you're tired separates smart riders from those who never seem to make much improvement.

4. Going hard each time you ride. Most rides should be at a relatively low heart rate of 65 to 80 percent of maximum to ensure you're rested for the occasional hard efforts that stimulate improvement. Cycling coach Tom Ehrhard points out that even the Australian national team, famous for its gut-busting interval workouts, "spends 60 to 90 percent of its total training time at heart rates below 120."

Michele Ferrari, coach of several European stars, states that "most recreational cyclists tend to ride the same all the time—too hard most days and too easy on hard days."

A slower pace burns body fat, increases aerobic capacity, and speeds recovery from harder workouts. On most rides, if you can't enjoy the scenery or talk with friends, slow down. If you return from every ride with dried white sweat on your helmet straps, you're overdoing it.

5. Not using a heart-rate monitor, or not using it enough. *Bicycling* magazine's Fitness Advisory Board was nearly unanimous when asked to name the most important training device of the 1990s: the heart-rate monitor. But many riders strap one on only for hard workouts. Instead, says Dr. Burke, use it when you're going easy. Set the upper alarm at 75 to 80 percent of your maximum heart rate. When it beeps, slow down. Think of your heart as a sports car engine and the monitor as a governor.

6. Avoiding dirt—or pavement. Ride both on-road and off-road. Although roadies and mountain bikers used to get along like two wary bulldogs, that's no longer true. Following the lead of the pros, nearly every serious cyclist spends time on fat and skinny tires. Riding off-road is an easy way to improve your bike handling. It increases your climbing power and gives you a break from traffic.

Conversely, road riding builds endurance with less stress, improves aerobic fitness, and smoothes out a pedal stroke made square by gnarly terrain. According to Colorado cycling coach and ultra-endurance athlete Skip Hamilton, "Most top mountain bike racers spend about 60 percent of their training time on road bikes." Surprised? If it works for the pros, it's a technique that can help recreational riders improve, too.

7. Doing nothing but riding. Cycling is improved by cycling. But when the weather or your schedule prevents riding, don't flop on the couch. Instead, consider other sports. Running, for instance, is easier on rainy days or when it gets dark early. Inline skating relieves monotony and can help your riding because both sports work similar muscles.

An alternate sport also diversifies your fitness. If all you do is ride, sprinting for first base at the company picnic will make you sore for a week. Run briefly twice a week, and you won't limp after you beat out the bunt.

8. Following a rigid ride schedule. Periodization (the process of dividing training into specific phases by weeks or months) is an effective technique for serious riders. But continual pressure to complete a specific workout each day can get old in a hurry. Sprints on Tuesday, endurance on Wednesday . . . wait a minute! Most cyclists ride to escape such pressure, not to be consumed by it. So especially if you're starting out in the sport, it's much better simply to ride like you feel. Just putting in time on the saddle will give you a solid base of conditioning. When the spirit moves you, sprint for a road sign or a bluebird on a fence. If you feel great, jam a few hills. If you're tired, spin gently, or take the day off.

9. Shunning hills. Befriend gravity. Choose a hilly route for your weekly hard ride and improvement is simple. A stiff climb boosts your heart rate into the stratosphere with little mental effort. It's much easier to hit 90 percent of max on a climb than when time-trialing on the flats. Great riders know this. It's why so many of them choose to live in hilly areas. Climbing is tough, but always remember—gravity makes you strong.

11
Fuel Your Cycling

In most recreational sports, eating is something you do afterward and, occasionally, beforehand. But in cycling, eating is often an important part of the activity. To most people who are new to riding, this is a surprise. So to bring you up to speed with one of the most important parts of the sport, here is a quick primer on the "why, when, what, and how" of eating, drinking, and cycling.

Why do you need to eat and drink on the bike?

Food replenishes the energy burned while riding. Every time you eat something, your body takes the food's carbohydrate (natural compounds known as starches and sugars) and stores it as fuel (glycogen) in your muscles and liver. You have enough stored glycogen to provide energy for 2 to 3 hours of riding. For longer efforts, however, you need to eat, or your glycogen stores will become depleted. When this occurs, less fuel reaches your muscles and brain. You feel weak and dizzy, a condition known in cycling as the bonk.

To avoid bonking, nibble food if you'll be cycling for 2 hours or longer. Also, never leave home without plenty of liquids. Cycling causes fluid loss through perspiration and respiration, so you must protect yourself against dehydration, a major contributor to fatigue.

When should you eat and drink?

The oldest advice for cyclists is still the best advice: Drink before you're thirsty and eat before you're hungry. If you wait for your body to tell you it needs nourishment, the energy won't be able to reach your muscles fast enough to prevent a drop-off in performance. One rule of thumb is to take a big swig from your bottle every 15 minutes. You should consume about 20 ounces per hour, which is the content of one standard-size bottle. Drink even more if it's hot and humid.

Another tenet is to allow yourself about an hour for digestion before riding. Then, if you'll be cycling for more than 2 hours, nibble periodically during the ride. During events, don't pig out at rest stops. Your digestive system needs lots of blood to process the contents of a full stomach, which leaves less for your muscles. The result can be cramping and indigestion. So here's another piece of time-tested advice: At rest stops, stuff your pockets, not your belly.

What should you eat and drink?

For fluid replacement on short rides, water works. But diluted fruit juice or commercial sports drinks are better, especially on longer outings. This is because they replenish energy-rich carbohydrate in addition to lost fluid. Drinks also are easier to ingest and digest than solids. According to studies, cyclists have the energy to ride nearly 13 percent farther when using a sports drink.

When you're off the bike, your diet should be 60 to 70 percent carbohydrate, 20 to 30 percent fat, and 10 to 15 percent protein. High-carbo foods include fruit, pasta, potatoes, rice, whole-grain breads, and vegetables.

Traditionally, the most popular on-bike food has been the banana. It's easy to eat, provides about 100 calories of carbohydrate, and replaces potassium, an important cramp-combating electrolyte lost via sweating. Other fresh fruit, such as pears (100 calories) and apples (80 calories), also provides carbohydrate, vitamins, minerals, and some fluid. Now, with the advent of so many varieties of energy bars, riders can choose their favorite tastes and textures for a concentrated energy source. Most bars supply around 200 calories, primarily from carbohydrate, plus vitamins and minerals.

Some riders also do well on higher-fat foods. Fat is accused of being an inefficient fuel source compared with carbohydrate, but it provides a longer burn that seems beneficial on rides that last several hours. Experiment to see how fat works for you. One easy-to-use source is the energy bars that provide a 40/30/30 ratio of carbohydrate/fat/protein.

Many long-distance cyclists who ride at a steady, moderate pace mix nuts, raisins, M&Ms, whole-grain cereal or granola, and other favorite munchies into a personalized concoction called gorp (good ol' raisins and peanuts). This is easy to nibble, and doing so delivers a steady flow of food energy.

Caffeine (coffee, cola, tea) may give you a temporary physical and mental boost. It has been shown in studies to promote the metabolism of fat for energy. But caffeine also causes fluid loss through urination, and its beneficial effects for cycling are reduced if you are a daily drinker.

How do you eat while riding?

The best place to carry food is in the rear pockets of a cycling jersey. To reach it, first grip the handlebar with one hand close to the stem to hold the bike steady. Then reach back with the other hand to fish around for what you want. Rear pockets can hold an extra bottle, too. Put it (or any heavy item) in the middle of the three pockets so it won't tug the jersey to the side.

Another approach is to snack during rest stops. It's common for touring cyclists to stash food in seatbags or rack trunks for roadside picnics. But as you now know, it's important to keep nibbling while riding between such stops.

Finally, don't forget the postride meal. As a cyclist, you'll regularly burn hundreds, if not thousands, of calories while exercising. So when you get home, you can guiltlessly enjoy an extra helping of your favorite food. In fact, eating a carbo-rich meal within an hour after finishing is the most effective way to replenish glycogen stores for the next day's ride. If it isn't practical to eat so soon, at least have another bottle of sports drink or one that's made for postexercise energy replenishment. Your muscles will thank you for it.

12

Find Time to Ride

Whether your goal is to ride for fitness and weight control or to participate in fast recreational rides with the local hotshots, one thing that is guaranteed to produce results is consistency. A well-designed training program will boost your speed, power, and endurance—the key elements of cycling performance. Look into the diary of almost any accomplished cyclist and you'll find weeks, months, and even years of persistent, methodical training.

But let's get real. You work for a living, often more than a mere 8 hours per day. You may have a spouse and maybe even a kid or two. You have social and community commitments, plus numerous other activities and responsibilities that seem to gobble every spare minute. Training program? A bigger concern is finding the time simply to ride with some regularity. In fact, *Bicycling* magazine surveys find that having enough time for cycling is rare among its readers.

With this in mind, here are some solutions to the time problem. Apply them to your unique situation and be creative in devising ways to fit cycling into your busy life.

Emphasize quality. With limited time to ride, it's important to make each minute count. One of the best ways is to invest in a heart-rate monitor (around $100 for a basic model). It helps you keep the bulk of each ride in the so-called target training zone, or about 60 to 85 percent of your maximum heart rate. This way, even outings as short as 30 minutes can enhance fitness. To make exertion fun, vary your riding with short time trials, intervals, sprints, and fast paceline work with your friends. All of these will boost your pulse far into the target zone, as will climbing hills. Fast, strenuous rides are important even for purely recreational riders because they build bike-handling skills as well as fitness. Don't overdo it, though, or you'll risk overtraining and fatigue. Always follow a hard ride with a day off or an easy spin at your 60-percent level to promote recovery.

Minimize your mileage. Sure, Tour de France racers train more than 400 miles a week and ultramarathon competitors might do nearly this much on a weekend, but your goals probably aren't in the transcontinental range. Don't feel pressured to maximize your mileage just because some riders do. For most lower-category recreational racers who compete in criteriums of 15 miles and road races of 60, about 150 well-planned training miles per week are plenty. If you want to ride centuries, consider this rule of thumb: You can generally handle a distance (or time on the bike) that is three times as long as your average ride. So once it's in the 30- to 35-mile range for a few weeks, you should be fine for a 100-miler. For beginners who have a half-century as their goal, a 15- to 20-mile daily average is sufficient. Remember that these figures describe average rides, so longer outings on Saturday and Sunday can balance shorter rides on weekdays.

Take days off. Everyone benefits from the recovery fostered by not riding 1 day each week, so even if you are forced to skip 2 or 3 days, don't get discouraged. Indeed, if missing a ride is inevitable, use this to your advantage by planning a more intense or longer workout before or after. Instead of feeling bad about not riding, you can feel good knowing that it's enabling you to rest and train better.

Commute. The oldest advice for limited-time cyclists is still the best: Ride your bike to your daily destination and use it for other transportation needs, too. No, these miles aren't likely to be high quality, given the stop-and-go nature of riding in town, but you can improve them with some ingenuity. The simplest way is to find a longer, less congested route home, and do some real training while you blow away the day's work stress. In not much longer than it takes to drive the same distance, you'll complete a decent workout and free your evening for other activities.

Ride after dark. Today's lighting systems for bicycles are amazing. At last, a bicycle rider can be as visible to traffic and see the road as well as a motorcyclist. This expands cycling potential to 24 hours a day, ridding you of anxiety about getting home in time to squeeze in a ride before sundown. That's a benefit worth the price ($100 and up) for a rechargeable lighting system. And there are other advantages. By not saddling up until twilight, you can miss rush-hour traffic, the air will be cleaner and cooler, and you can enjoy a beautiful sight that your unlit counterparts are sprinting home to avoid: sunset. Use a taillight, wear reflective clothing, and decorate your bike with reflective tape. You'll be such a sight that most drivers will give you more room than they ever do in daylight.

Ride at dawn. If you're a morning person, cycling can take place in the day's first light, using a lighting system if necessary. The advantages include cool, calm air, minimal traffic, and the satisfaction of knowing you've had your ride no matter what else the day brings. This requires going to sleep earlier, however, to avoid fatigue that could undermine both cycling and job performance.

Get out at lunch. When you're forced to fit your ride into an hour, you have the impetus to pedal briskly. The result should be lots of fitness for the time spent. Don't fail to sandwich a brief warmup and cooldown around the harder and faster portion of each ride. Of course, to ride during lunch, you need suitable roads nearby (a park may be available if you work in a city), a way to clean up afterward, and a safe place to keep your bike. Make up for the missed meal by snacking on wholesome foods at your desk an hour before and after riding.

Cycle inside. When the rain rattles or the icy wind whips, put your bike on an indoor trainer. It's not the same as riding outside, but it's close enough if you use it right. Don't just sit there working up a light sweat. Instead, wear your heart-rate monitor and strive for the same intensity you get on the road. Warm up for 10 minutes, do 20 to 30 minutes of interval-type efforts that drive your pulse to the 85-percent-of-max range, then cool down for 5 minutes. Bingo—a beneficial workout in less than 45 minutes. Even when the weather is fine but your daily schedule isn't, inside cycling can be done at any hour to help maintain consistency.

Plan. Use these tips to safeguard precious time.

- If you realize your bike needs an adjustment, make it immediately upon returning from the ride so you won't need to delay the next one.

- Use butyl rather than porous latex inner tubes so you only need to inflate them once per week.

- Install Kevlar-belted tires, liners, or leak-sealing tubes to prevent rides from being shortened by flats.

- Lay out your riding clothes at night so you won't waste time looking for anything.

- Prepare your preride or on-bike food and drink in advance.

- Establish a routine so that everything surrounding each ride is streamlined and efficient.

Set goals. When you have the date of an important club ride, race, century, tour, or other event circled on the calendar, you won't have difficulty motivating yourself to find riding opportunities. As the crucial day nears, you can justify arranging other parts of your life around cycling for a change. After all, you've earned it with your dedication. Afterward, reduce your cycling and take care of things you ignored, then identify another goal to build toward. This pattern helps vary the routine and provides chances to enjoy your improved fitness and skill. There's nothing like feeling progress to keep you interested in staying with it.

Oh, and one more thing—keep it fun! For most riders, cycling is so enjoyable that they can't do enough. Use all of the above tips to make sure that it stays that way. Don't feel pressured to ride at any cost, don't continually thrash yourself until your heart rate redlines, and never let it become monotonous. Above all, don't get down when something in your busy life stymies your plans. Be flexible, and keep your perspective. When cycling is fun, you'll always be finding new ways to fit it in.

PART THREE

Getting Good

13
Principles of Training

When Jerry Watson was in his midthirties, he was working 80-hour weeks as a stock broker in New York City and training on his bike for 2 hours every day. By the end of that season, he suffered from fatigue, heat intolerance, and vision problems. Eventually, he was diagnosed with multiple sclerosis. How could a young, healthy, hard-charging competitive rider suddenly become so ill? Apparently, it was a combination of racing and job stress, plus injuries he'd suffered earlier in a car accident.

Can too much cycling make you sick? Even for fitness cyclists, can lots of riding combine with typical life stresses to suppress the immune system, leading not to better health but to the colds, flu, bronchitis, and similar ailments that sometimes strike amateur racers and fast recreational riders?

Cyclists have asked such questions for years. The first scientific evidence hinting at the danger of riding too much came from a study of 17,000 Harvard alumni by Ralph Paffenberger Jr., M.D. He found that the death rate was a quarter to a third lower among men expending 2,000 calories per week in exercise. But at higher levels of exercise— around 4,000 calories per week—the mortality rate rose.

Aside from this pioneering study, most conclusions about overtraining have been based on anecdotal evidence. Ed Burke, Ph.D., cycling physiologist and director of the exercise-science program at the University of Colorado at Colorado Springs, has worked with elite cyclists for 2 decades. He says he's become convinced that "chronic, hard, endurance training can depress the immune system. It isn't a healthy situation."

Hard Evidence

Until recently, there was little evidence of risks beyond the one landmark study and some educated guesses. Then came the results of a test performed in Poland. Fifteen young racers were examined, then rechecked after 6 months of intense training and racing (averaging more than 300 miles per week, much of it at extreme effort). Not surprisingly, tests showed marked improvement in their abilities to ride stronger and longer. But lab work revealed a significant decrease in several immune system components. As they'd become fitter, their resistance to illness had declined.

In Australia, researchers severely overtrained five male runners by subjecting them to two intense interval sessions each day for 10 days. After only 6 days, the runners showed significant reductions in the special types of cells that battle illness, as well as progressively declining amounts of body chemicals and substances that help prevent fatigue.

The message is clear. Riding too much or too hard can not only harm performance, it might even threaten your health—and ultimately your longevity. The question is: How much riding can you do before it becomes too much?

Moderation Means Safety

The same studies that reveal the harm of overtraining also demonstrate that moderate cycling doesn't weaken your immune system. In fact, most of the markers of a strong immune system are boosted by moderate training.

But defining moderation is tough because individual reactions to cycling vary greatly. A fast century might strengthen one rider's immune system while plunging other cyclists into illness. That's why professional racers are successful only if they have iron constitutions. The demands of high-intensity riding and lots of miles weed out racers with relatively weak systems.

Moderate cycling is also relative to the rest of your life. Pro cyclists can complete exhausting multiday races because they think of little else but riding, eating, and sleeping. Their other needs are met by a team of support people, keeping their overall stress tolerable.

Now consider typical recreational cyclists like Watson. They train a fraction of the miles logged by a pro. But they often have demanding jobs, families, and maybe stressful auto commutes on crowded roads. No mechanic maintains their bikes. Is it possible to overtrain on 150 miles a week when pros routinely ride 500? You bet it is. In fact, when total stress is considered, many recreational riders may be working harder than the stars.

Cycling coach Tom Ehrhard agrees. "Stressors such as job and marital problems, or a poor diet, combine with training to form a total stress equation," he says. "Keep this below your individual tolerance point, and you'll be healthy and react to training by improving. Beyond your tolerance point, you'll be subjected to a fascinating array of sicknesses such as mononucleosis and chronic fatigue syndrome, as well as more colds and flu."

Signs of Doing Too Much

How do you know if you're going over the edge? Here are the signals of overtraining.

Poor performance. If your fitness worsens in spite of riding more, it's almost certainly getting worse *because* you're riding more. Take some time off, maintaining fitness with easy aerobic activities such as hiking or swimming at a heart rate below 70 percent of your maximum. Ehrhard recommends "putting a big cog on your cassette and noodling up hills instead of pushing." Although the rest that's needed to recover varies with individual riders, you might try scheduling 2 or 3 rest days each week when you resume riding.

General fatigue. Day-long exhaustion or lethargy is a sure sign. If you don't have the energy to mow the lawn, you have no business hammering with your cycling pals.

Negative emotions. A ground-breaking study in the 1970s by William Morgan, Ph.D., showed that the mood profiles of overtrained athletes are reversed from those of normal people. Instead of being high in vigor and energy, overtrained athletes were high in anxiety, fatigue, and lethargy. In fact, Dr. Morgan commented that he'd never seen an overtrained athlete who wasn't clinically depressed.

You don't need a psychologist to tell you when you're fried. Friends and family will usually let you know about personality changes. If you feel irritable and grouchy, short-tempered at work and emotionally unstable, you could be spending too much time on your bike.

Vague physical complaints. "Sore throats or odd sicknesses can be leading indicators of chronic stress," says Ehrhard. So can sore muscles. Unlike impact sports such as running, cycling doesn't normally produce leg soreness. So if your gams are aching, you're overdoing it. Chronic diarrhea or heartburn can mean that your system is so overworked by riding that it can't process food properly.

Disruption of your normal sleep rhythm. Overtrained cyclists often fall asleep easily but wake abruptly in the early morning. By 10:00 A.M., they're ready for a nap. Poor sleep means it's time to reduce riding.

Elevated heart rate. It's useful to take your pulse each morning just after waking up. If you see an increase of 10 percent for several days, it probably means your body isn't adapting to the stresses of cycling.

An overpowering desire to buy a new bike. Severe bike lust might mean you're no longer enjoying riding for the sake of riding. You could be bored and tired, subconsciously craving a different bike to bring freshness to your cycling.

How to Train Your Heart

How can you be sure your cycling program is good for your heart while improving your performance and enjoyment? The key to increasing fitness is knowing your maximum heart rate, then riding at the specific percentages described below. The best way to find your max is to have a stress test or max VO_2 test in supervised conditions at a medical facility. But with your doctor's permission, you can test yourself by using a heart-rate monitor and climbing a long, steep hill. Simply push until you think you can't go any harder, then sprint like the world championship is on the line. The pulse you reach will be very close to your max.

Beware of the old formula that says to subtract your age from 220. This can be wildly inaccurate. If it's off by 8 to 10 beats for you, the training formulas will make your efforts too easy for the best improvement, or so hard that you may become overtrained. The secret is to mix up the type of training you do, because cycling at different intensities affects the heart in different ways. Essentially, your heart works in three zones of effort.

Easiest is an aerobic intensity of about 65 to 80 percent of maximum heart rate (MHR), a pace that you can sustain for several hours. You don't need a heart-rate monitor to identify when you're in this zone. The effort feels easy to moderate and you can easily carry on a conversation. Second, and harder, is a pace that develops your lactate threshold, about 85 to 90 percent of MHR. It's an intensity that you can sustain for an hour or less. It'll feel hard. Duplicate it by time-trialing 10 miles as hard as you can go for the distance. Third, your heart is capable of all-out short efforts that reach 100 percent of MHR. These develop your max VO_2, short for maximal oxygen consumption. This riding intensity feels Herculean.

A well-rounded training program hits all three zones several times a week. You have two choices. There's the low-tech method: Just ride and hopefully do enough at each level of intensity to improve. So in a typical week you'd cruise for aerobic work, do a time trial or an extended climb to raise your lactate threshold, and do a couple of hard jams with friends to create max VO$_2$ improvement. Too haphazard for you? Then get a heart-rate monitor and follow this three-part training program to make sure your ticker gets the full range of effort each week.

Aerobic. This is the easiest zone to monitor. Just spend about 80 percent of your weekly riding time cruising at a moderate but enjoyable effort, 65 to 80 percent of MHR. This is basic training for heart health.

Lactate threshold. Get your heart rate into the 85 to 90 percent range twice a week for 10 to 20 minutes by riding the local club time trial or climbing a long hill. Or, do two or three repeats of 10 minutes each. Keep the effort steady and don't sprint at the end. Plan your energy expenditure so you feel as if you could do one more repeat if you had to. The result will be a higher heart rate at which lactic acid floods your muscles and makes you slow down. You'll be able to ride harder or climb faster for longer periods.

Max VO$_2$. These are the hardest efforts in your heart workout arsenal, but just a few minutes once a week pays big dividends in strength and power. After a good warmup, do three repeats of 3 minutes each at a pace so hard you can't last longer. This should push you to 91 to 100 percent of your max heart rate. Roll easily for 3 to 5 minutes between repeats. Or you can just jam hard and fast three times for a couple of minutes whenever you feel like it in the middle of an aerobically paced ride. Steep hills are natural for this.

14
Instant Improvement

There's no denying the effectiveness of training plans and season-long goals. But wouldn't it be nice if you could become a better cyclist this afternoon, even if the improvement were only a tiny one?

Of course it would. And of course you can. Below is a collection of great advice to help you achieve this small but satisfying goal. Most of these tips outline proven bike-handling and riding techniques. Others focus on posture, discipline, and pre- and postride habits. But the one thing commonly shared is that they all can be used immediately—before, during, or after your next ride—to gain more speed, comfort, and confidence.

1. Instead of actively drawing air into your lungs and then passively letting it out as in normal breathing, do the opposite: Actively push air out and then passively let it in. This technique not only increases airflow, it helps you breathe evenly instead of panting.

2. If you're riding into a major headwind, don't fight to keep your speed. In terms of pedaling effort, a cyclist who travels 18 mph through calm air has to work about twice as hard to maintain this pace into a 10-mph headwind. So use windy days as an opportunity to slow down and work on your pedaling form.

3. Thirty minutes before a 2-hour ride, eat one energy bar and drink 12 to 16 ounces of water. This will top off your fuel stores and help postpone the fatiguing effects of dehydration. You'll have one of your best rides ever.

4. If you have a wristwatch with a countdown timer, set it to beep every 15 minutes on your next ride. This is your signal to take a slug of water. Ride with the watch until drinking at regular intervals becomes second nature. Dehydration is the most preventable cause of cycling fatigue.

5. Surprise your friends with an occasional breakaway or sprint toward a landmark. The thrill of the chase gets competitive juices flowing, enlivens group rides, and improves the quality of your workout.

6. Increase your stability during road descents by pedaling instead of coasting. Staying in a high gear also allows you to accelerate if the situation calls for sudden speed. Off-road, shift to the middle or big ring for descents to keep the chain from slapping against the frame or derailing.

7. When standing on a climb, rise from the saddle just as your dominant leg is beginning its downstroke, and apply extra pedaling pressure. This will help you keep your speed during the transition from sitting to standing.

8. Ride familiar courses in the opposite direction. Besides the refreshing difference in scenery, your workout will also change because the challenges come at you in a new order.

9. Don't be afraid of the big chainring. Wait until you're warmed up and you have a tailwind or a long downgrade, then go for it. Pushing a big gear helps to develop strength and gives you the thrill of power and speed. Even if you're not competitive, you'll benefit when the wind turns against you or when the road takes an upward slant.

10. To keep from skidding during off-road descents, apply the front brake firmly. There's more weight on this tire, so you can maintain more control. Just make sure to stay low and back on the saddle to keep from flipping forward. Also be careful on curves, where front braking can cause a sideways wipeout.

11. Shift 20 percent more often. With the advent of index shifting and convenient handlebar-mounted levers, changing gears is all but automatic. But most road riders still don't do enough of it. To be as efficient an engine as possible and minimize knee strain, shift often to keep your cadence at about 90 revolutions per minute. To calculate this, count how many times your right foot comes around the pedal circle in 30 seconds, then multiply by two.

12. Adjust your mountain bike's tire pressure because you're probably riding with too much of it off-road. Excess air reduces traction and the cushioning ability of fat tires. You can usually gain more control by riding at around 30 to 35 psi. (Adjust to your weight, riding style, and surface conditions. Too little pressure in rough terrain can result in pinch or "snakebite" punctures.)

13. On long rides, stand for 1 minute out of every 20. This stretches your body and relieves saddle pressure, helping you feel fresher longer.

14. To delay fatigue during hard, sustained pedaling, learn to "float" each leg every three or four strokes. Let your foot fall without pushing down, thereby relaxing the muscles and allowing better circulation. Legendary French time trialist Jacques Anquetil popularized this technique.

15. Don't brake in a paceline. This slows you too much, opens a gap, and can cause a dangerous chain reaction. If you begin to overtake the rider in front, ease pedal pressure or move slightly to the side to catch more wind. Once you've lost enough speed, smoothly resume pedaling.

16. Gain a few free inches every time you go from standing to sitting. Just push your bike forward by straightening your arms as you drop to the saddle.

17. Ride with a purpose. If today's ride is with a group, practice your drafting skills by organizing a paceline. If you're going solo, focus on low-gear sprints to develop your spin, or hill repeats to improve your climbing. If this is an easy day, work on cornering, no-hands riding, or other skills that won't tax your cardiovascular system. Even if you're not on a training schedule, select one objective before you get on your bike. This keeps you from pedaling "junk miles" that don't improve skill.

18. Keep your elbows bent throughout the ride. Many cyclists begin with the proper posture, but slip out of position as they fatigue. This tires you even more. To check your form, watch your shadow or your reflection in large windows that you pass.

19. To ride more safely through sandy or gravelly corners on your road bike, approach the turn from the widest angle (traffic permitting). This allows you to ride a straighter line through the loose stuff. Once past it, resume turning. The key is to minimize leaning on these surfaces.

20. To help cultivate a fast, smooth spin, intentionally stay in lower gears during one ride each week.

21. To ride your mountain bike through mud bogs, shift to a lower gear and slide back on the saddle so the front wheel won't plow in. Keep pedaling to maintain balance and forward progress. Use the straightest line because turning steals momentum. If you're light, you can "float" through. If you're heavy, you'll sink to the bottom and have to power and churn your way to the other side.

22. Cross railroad tracks near the side of the road. It's usually less worn there than in the center, so the risk of wheel damage is reduced. Help matters by rising slightly off the saddle so you can coast across the tracks with the bike free to chatter beneath you. Always cross with your wheels perpendicular to the rails, and be extremely careful of riding over tracks or anything metal if it's wet. Never lean or turn, or you'll slip down as if on ice.

23. Start a cycling diary. This document of your rides doesn't have to be elaborate, time-consuming, or expensive. All you need is a notebook to jot pertinent data (miles ridden, average speed, terrain, weather, how you felt, what you ate) each day. Recording your impressions helps keep you enthusiastic about riding. And as time goes by, the diary will let you objectively analyze and learn from what you've done right (and what you've done wrong).

24. If the chain accidentally derails onto the bottom bracket or off the outside of the large chainring, you can often pop it back on by moving the left shift lever while pedaling gently. Don't automatically stop to put the chain back on by hand. If this technique doesn't work, don't force it and cause damage.

25. Look for telltale changes in ground color when cycling off-road. In dry climates, for instance, darker soil usually harbors more moisture and better traction.

26. Unpackage, slice, and rewrap your snacks before riding. This can save time and increase safety when you want to pull out food to eat while pedaling. It's especially helpful in winter when you're riding with full-finger gloves.

27. To power over obstacles, loose ground, and other off-road debris, use the strength of your upper body to dynamically pulse the rear tire. Do this by standing, bending your elbows, lowering your head toward the stem, and pulling back and up on the handlebar at the beginning of each pedal stroke. It's sort of a seesaw rowing action that switches on your power.

28. When there's a strong crosswind from the left, you naturally lean into it to keep a straight line. But when cars pass and momentarily block the wind, it may cause you to steer into their lane. Anticipate this and prevent it by keeping your elbows and grip relaxed so that your response time to the changing forces can be quicker.

29. If an off-road route frequently requires you to pick up and carry (portage) your bike, carry as much of your food, tools, and other accessories as is practical on your body, where the weight won't be as much of a detriment. Putting water bottles and tools into a fanny pack instead of on your bike will minimize upper-body fatigue from continual lifting.

30. To pick up an extra mile per hour (or more), tell yourself to pedal faster instead of harder. The former helps quicken your pedal cadence, while the latter tends to tense your muscles and increase your mental strain.

15
Train for a Century

Maybe. Could have. Should have. If only.

Forget these excuses right now. You won't need to spit them out on century day if you follow this plan for riding 100 miles.

One hundred miles! Is this a joke? Not at all. Despite the fact that a century ride sounds impossible to most new riders, thousands of cyclists accomplish the feat each year, including many who are making their first assault on a triple-digit distance.

If you're not thinking about riding a 100-miler now, you will be. In most parts of the country, bike clubs traditionally hold century rides in the fall, though early spring is the main season on the West Coast. These are often gala events, with well-stocked rest stops, a postride feast, and T-shirts or patches for all finishers. For many cyclists, it's the highlight of the season.

But for those who are unprepared, the challenge of a century comes not from the miles or the terrain, but from trying to coax a poorly nourished or undertrained body past its limits. That's the wrong challenge, and it's not very fun or rewarding.

With proper training, however, you can face 100 miles being fit, rested, and well-fed. This doesn't mean the ride will be too easy. The distance will still be a challenge, but you'll have given yourself a fair chance. You'll be more likely to swap success stories at the finish instead of excuses.

Here are some of the best hints and advice on completing this classic endurance event. Realize, too, that many century rides offer shorter distances if 100 miles is too much too soon for you. There may be a metric century (62 miles), a half-century (50), or a quarter-century (25). The following tips still apply; simply adjust mileages accordingly.

The Programs

The basis of your preparation will be one of *Bicycling* magazine's two proven 10-week training programs. This will help you build your endurance slowly and methodically.

"A Program to Survive" is for cyclists attempting their first century. It's geared for riders who've been averaging 45 to 50 miles per week or less. If you've been riding more, you can increase the recommended distances slightly or jump to the tougher program.

Follow "A Program to Thrive" on page 66 if your weekly mileage is higher than 75. This schedule will help you finish the century with strength to spare. It can also be used by century veterans to train for a personal record.

In both charts, "easy" means a leisurely ride, "pace" means matching the speed you want to maintain during the century, and "brisk" means riding faster than your century speed.

Whichever schedule you use, you'll need to find training time during the week. Try commuting, riding at lunch, or even using a stationary trainer. It's crucial to ride at least 5 days per week.

A Program to Survive

WEEK	MON	TUES	WED	THUR	FRI	SAT	SUN	MILEAGE WEEKLY
	Easy	Pace	Brisk		Pace	Pace	Pace	
1	6	10	12	Off	10	30	9	77
2	7	11	13	Off	11	34	10	86
3	8	13	15	Off	13	38	11	98
4	8	14	17	Off	14	42	13	108
5	9	15	19	Off	15	47	14	119
6	11	15	21	Off	15	53	16	131
7	12	15	24	Off	15	59	18	143
8	13	15	25	Off	15	65	20	153
9	15	15	25	Off	15	65	20	155
10	15	15	25	Off	10	5 (easy)	Century	170

If you do skip a day, make sure it's not a Saturday. This is the most important part of the schedule. Riding longer distances each weekend is the key to century training. If rain or some other calamity disrupts your Saturday ride, use Sunday as your long day.

As you get in shape, you may be tempted to increase your weekly mileage beyond the recommendations. Small increases are okay, but don't drastically hike your mileage. The schedules use a 10 to 12 percent weekly increase, which boosts fitness while guarding against over-training, fatigue, and injury.

Finally, feel free to adjust the schedule to your lifestyle. Following a makeshift version of this program is more beneficial than abandoning your training schedule because you can't adhere exactly to the plan. It's okay to switch your off day, swap "brisk" and "pace" days, or make other changes, as long as you follow these guidelines:

■ Take at least 1 day off per week, but no more than 2. (Remember, easy riding helps you recover better than inactivity.)

■ "Easy" is a steady spin at a pace slower than your century pace. "Pace" is the speed and effort you will try to maintain during the century. "Brisk" is 1 to 2 mph faster than your century pace.

■ Make sure that a high-mileage ride is always followed by a relatively easy day.

A Program to Thrive

WEEK	MON	TUES	WED	THUR	FRI	SAT	SUN	WEEKLY MILEAGE
	Easy	Pace	Brisk		Pace	Pace	Pace	
1	10	12	14	Off	12	40	15	103
2	10	13	15	Off	13	44	17	112
3	10	15	17	Off	15	48	18	123
4	11	16	19	Off	16	53	20	135
5	12	18	20	Off	18	59	22	149
6	13	19	23	Off	19	64	24	162
7	14	20	25	Off	20	71	27	177
8	16	20	27	Off	20	75	29	187
9	17	20	30	Off	20	75	32	194
10	19	20	30	Off	10	5 (easy)	Century	184

- If you miss a daily mileage goal, add the mileage somewhere else during that same week. The 10 percent total mileage increase is crucial.

- The final-week taper is important. You'll start feeling lots of energy, but control yourself during training, and save it for the big day.

- If your century is on a Saturday, move back the final week's schedule one day. (Take Wednesday off and ride 10 miles on Thursday and 5 miles on Friday.)

Eat to Succeed

During training, eat a diet of 60 to 70 percent carbohydrate, 20 to 30 percent fat, and 10 to 15 percent protein. This gives you a good supply of carbo, cycling's main fuel. Then, in the 3 to 6 days before the ride, eat at least 75 percent of your calories as carbohydrate. Go for pasta, potatoes, vegetables, grains, fruit, Chinese and Mexican food, bread, and high-energy snacks. This "carbo-loading" will ensure that you have plenty of energy packed in your body. Also, drink plenty of nonalcoholic and caffeine-free liquids to fully hydrate and aid carbo digestion.

Don't overeat on the morning of the ride. Limit your breakfast to 800 calories or less. Give yourself 1 hour before the ride for every 200 calories you eat. For example, a 400-calorie breakfast of cereal, juice, and a bagel should be eaten about 2 hours before the start of the ride.

During the ride, nibble on snacks such as bananas, fig cookies, or energy bars. Some riders like to eat every 20 miles, some prefer every 10, others go by time. You should have discovered what works for you during your long training rides.

Don't pig out at the rest stops. It's better to munch lightly and steadily instead of stuffing yourself. Large amounts of food divert blood from your working muscles to your stomach, which can weaken and even nauseate you.

Fluid is as important as food. In addition to drinking extra during the days leading up to the ride, have three glasses of water, juice, or sports drink during the morning. Once you're on the bike, a good general rule is to empty at least one standard-size bottle (about 20 ounces) each hour. If it's hot or humid, two bottles per hour is not unreasonable.

Energy drinks are a good substitute for water and a portion of the food calories you need. These products are quick sources of carbo as well as some important nutrients, such as electrolytes that help prevent cramping. Some riders like to have one bottle of energy drink and one of water, which works better for washing down sweet food. Experiment in training. Some energy drinks may taste and perform better for you than others. Century rest stops often have energy drinks so you can refill your bottle.

Finally, remember the golden rule of long-distance cycling: Eat before you're hungry and drink before you're thirsty. This will keep your energy and hydration levels high and enable a strong ride.

Ride Strategies

What you do the day of the ride can be as important as your months of training. Here are some tips to see you to the finish.

1. Make sure your bike is in good mechanical shape and is properly geared for the course. Plan for a tune-up about a week before the ride. Don't change any equipment (especially the saddle) unless you'll be able to check it out during several training rides.

2. Lay out your riding clothes the night before the century. This will keep you from a frantic and stressful early-morning search for your lucky socks. Also, inflate your tires to full recommended pressure (imprinted on the sidewall).

3. Check the weather report. If it may be cool and rainy, take leg warmers, arm warmers, and a rain jacket. Warmers are better than wearing tights and a long-sleeve jersey because you can peel them off and tuck them into your jersey pockets if the temperature rises.

4. Stretch before you ride, even if you never do so in training. Cold legs will eventually warm up, but during such a long ride, your upper body can stiffen from inactivity. Also stretch at rest stops, or even on the bike. Every 30 minutes, stand on the pedals, arch your back, and stretch your legs. Do slow neck rolls and shoulder shrugs. Vary your riding position by moving your hands from atop the handlebar to the brake lever hoods and drops (or bar-ends of a mountain bike or hybrid). This also helps to prevent muscle fatigue.

5. Don't stop for more than 10 minutes. Longer breaks can make you stiff and sluggish.

6. Divide the ride into segments. Think of it as four 25-mile rides, or two 50-milers. Some cyclists like to ride a negative split—faster in the second half than the first. This prevents them from riding too hard too soon. Others plan their strategy around a course's biggest hill. Talk to the organizers and other riders about possible strategies.

7. If you become tired, don't think about how many miles remain. Make each rest stop your new goal. Concentrate on your form and on drinking and eating. Talking with other riders is one way to take your mind off the exertion. Drafting them can give you the physical and mental boost you need to maintain your pace.

8. Don't ride "beyond" yourself. Centuries inevitably divide into groups of riders. Don't blow up trying to stay with a fast pack, especially early on. Let yourself drift back until you're in the company of riders who share your pace. Similarly, don't dawdle. If you feel reined in, break away or latch onto a passing pack. It's much easier to ride a century in a group than solo, though for some riders the feeling of accomplishment isn't as great.

9. When you complete the century, perform this important maneuver. Depending on your bike-handling ability, it can be done while rolling or stopped. Keep your left hand on the handlebar. Bend your right elbow and place your hand between your shoulder blades. Then, give yourself a pat on the back. You deserve it.

16
Winter Workouts

In winter, bad weather and early darkness combine to deliver a powerful one-two punch to every cyclist. It's impossible to maintain on-bike training in most parts of the country, but doing nothing will destroy the fitness built all summer. Studies prove that after about 1 month of inactivity, even the best-conditioned athletes lose most of their fitness.

Looked at another way, though, a shortage of cycling time after the autumnal equinox can be a blessing in disguise. If you continue to ride through the winter, chances are great that you'll be mentally and physically tired when spring rolls around. So instead of moaning about winter, think of it as an ideal time to recharge your eagerness and develop the types of fitness that cycling doesn't provide.

With this in mind, here's the challenge: Emerge from winter with your fitness not only intact but improved and your enthusiasm for cycling sky-high. And do it all in a reasonable amount of time. Let's say you have 6 hours per week for exercise—4 days when you can devote 1 hour, and a fifth day when you can devote 2. Furthermore, because your time is limited, you can't afford to waste any of it commuting to a health club. All of your workouts must be done at or near your home.

As difficult as it may seem, there is a way to succeed even with such constraints. Here's how.

Set goals. Know what you want to accomplish before you start. For instance, maybe you'd like to keep from gaining weight or perhaps lose a few pounds. This would mean devoting a substantial portion of your winter training program to calorie-burning aerobic activities. At the same time, you wouldn't want to sacrifice any of your strength or cardiovascular capacity, so weight training and hill running might be in order. Whatever your goals, remember that for mental as well as physical reasons, you may benefit from a break from cycling. You don't want to stop riding altogether, but this is a great time to experiment with other sports.

Schedule wisely. Assess your daily commitments to realistically determine when you can exercise. If you have a long lunch hour, you might be able to exercise outside on mild days. If you don't have any free time until late afternoon, you may have to resort to riding on an indoor trainer. Don't try to squeeze in workouts when time is too tight. That only leads to stress and frustration.

Keep it simple. Maintain your perspective. You're not training for the Tour de France. Your program doesn't have to be rigid or complicated. It should be enjoyable. And on a limited time budget, the simpler it is, the better.

Essential Components

During the off-season, de-emphasize cycling. You'll be that much more eager to ride when spring comes. But if you neglect the bike completely all winter, you'll start up in April with weak legs, a tender rear end, and an inefficient pedal stroke. The trick is to ride just enough to maintain your cycling fitness. In the dark days of midwinter, this means pedaling on an indoor trainer where it's warm and dry.

But even the most dedicated riders may find it difficult to ride inside. One way to keep pedaling in easy-to-swallow doses is to use the trainer as a way to warm up and cool down from other activities such as weight training or running. This approach not only gives you the benefits of different activities, it also keeps your legs familiar with turning the crankset even though there's the all-important mental relief from cycling workouts.

Of course, if you can get out on the road occasionally, do it. But ride at a moderate-to-leisurely pace with friends (if possible), and make the main goal to have fun. If the roads in your area tend to stay messy with moisture and grit, install fenders. A mountain bike works great for riding on winter roads because the knobby tires provide good traction, and their higher rolling resistance gives you an ample workout even at slower speeds, which reduce the windchill.

Take that mountain bike off-road, too, if conditions allow. You can improve your bike-handling skills, build power, and have a blast riding dirt roads and trails. When you get to sections too tough to ride, hop off and run with the bike. This uses different muscles and boosts your heart rate.

Resistance Training

Cyclists need strong upper bodies to stabilize their riding position and reduce fatigue on extended treks. But riding by itself won't develop this type of torso. Resistance training is necessary, and winter is the ideal time to get strong. Here's what you'll need for an at-home winter weight-training program.

1. An indoor trainer for your bike

2. A pullup bar

3. An inexpensive barbell set totaling 110 pounds

4. A sturdy bench

Begin each workout with a 15-minute warmup on the trainer. Then do the following exercises. Choose a light weight—one that allows you to perform 10 to 20 repetitions without a helper. Begin with one set for each exercise. Add a second set as you get stronger, and add more weight when you can exceed 20 reps. If you're inexperienced in weight training, consult a book that shows how to do the different exercises correctly, or better yet, get professional instruction from a personal trainer.

Pullup. In this day of fancy fitness machines, the simple pullup is still one of the best overall upper-body exercises for cyclists. It works the muscles that pull on the handlebar when you're sprinting or climbing. You can derive even more benefit by varying your grip on different sets: palms away, palms toward you, narrow grip, wide grip. If you're a real Tarzan and can do more than 20 pullups, tie a barbell plate to your waist for added resistance.

Bench press. This basic upper-body exercise strengthens the muscles that support your torso while riding. If your arms and shoulders ache during long rides, benches will help. But don't aim for heavy poundage. Use a moderate weight and concentrate on good form through the full range of motion.

Upright row. This barbell exercise develops the trapezius muscles that help protect your neck in a fall. It also strengthens your shoulder girdle, thus guarding against collarbone fractures and shoulder separations. Stand upright holding a barbell in both hands, palms facing your body in a narrow grip, hands a few inches from the center of the barbell. Extend your arms down in front of you and then lift the barbell up, pulling it toward your head until it's no higher than chest level. As a bonus, the added strength you'll derive from doing upright rows will help support the weight of your head and helmet on long rides, combating neck pain and fatigue. Use light weights for this one and don't cheat—keep your upper body still.

Pushup. This is another vital but unglamorous exercise. Pushups strengthen your triceps, the arm muscles that help support your upper body when you're leaning on the handlebar. Pushups are a good supplement to bench presses because they work the same muscles at a different angle. As with pullups, vary your hand spacing.

Squat. This is the best exercise for developing leg power because squats work your quadriceps, hips, and lower back—the same muscles that produce your pedal stroke. Hold the barbell with your palms facing forward and place it behind your neck. Keep your feet hip-width apart, with your toes forward and slightly out. Though sometimes maligned as a cause of injury, squats are safe if you follow four rules.

- Use light weights and do high repetitions (15 to 30).

- Squat until your thighs are parallel to the floor, producing close to the same knee bend as when pedaling. Don't go lower.

- Maintain correct form. Keep your back flat, your head up, and your chest out. Don't bounce at the bottom of the movement.

- Stop one rep short of maximum if you don't have a helper. Otherwise, you could get stuck in the squatting position.

Crunch. This exercise builds strong abdominals. While these muscles aren't used in cycling, they are crucial for supporting and aligning your back. If you experience lower-back pain, especially on longer rides, crunches may be the solution. End your weight workout by cooling down on the trainer for about 5 minutes.

Aerobic Activities

For variety and well-rounded cardiovascular development, cyclists should participate in other aerobic activities during the off-season.

Running is especially useful in winter. It's not only possible to run in adverse conditions, it's also easy to get a good workout in a relatively short time. In addition, running strengthens the calves and hamstrings—two areas that cycling overlooks. Hard uphill running, on the other hand, benefits the same muscles cycling uses.

Running has its disadvantages—chiefly the possibility of injury. To avoid being sidelined, invest in high-quality shoes with good support. On steep downhills, walk to protect your knees. And most important, start your running program gradually. You might begin by doing 4 miles this way: Walk 2, run 1, and walk the last 1. Each time out, increase the running segment by a half-mile until you're trotting the full distance.

If you have access to a pool and the time to use it, swimming is one of the best total-body conditioners. You'll develop upper-body strength and flexibility as well as cardiovascular power. It's great for learning breath control, too.

Cross-country skiing and snowshoeing with poles are great fitness activities if you live where there's ample snow. In fact, the poling motion affords the same benefits as spending an equal amount of time in the weight room. If you're skeptical, just wait until you feel those tender triceps the morning after. Greg LeMond, the three-time Tour de France champion who lives in Minnesota, is a strong advocate, saying, "If you did a good ski program for 3 months and rode a trainer two or three times a week, you'd be ready to race with only 3 weeks of road training at the beginning of the season."

Other Sports

No winter program is complete without including some fun sports to hone coordination and agility. Try the old standbys: basketball, volleyball, soccer, handball, and racquetball. Or go for more exotic activities like aerobic dance or karate. The more time you spend riding your bike in the summer, the more your basic coordination and agility tend to deteriorate during the winter.

Weekly Schedule

Here's a sample workout schedule for an average cyclist who works daily from 9:00 A.M. to 5:00 P.M. and also has family responsibilities. In keeping with the ground rules, he has just 6 hours per week to exercise. This includes 1 hour 3 days a week after work when it's too dark to ride outside, another hour on Saturday morning, and 2 hours on Sunday.

Monday: Rest.

Tuesday: Spend 30 to 45 minutes running or doing some other type of aerobic activity. For the rest of the hour, ride the indoor trainer at a moderate pace.

Wednesday: Warm up for 15 minutes on the trainer. Do resistance exercises for 35 minutes. Then cool down on the trainer for 10 minutes.

Thursday: Warm up with light stretching, jogging, or spinning on the trainer. Then participate in an active sport such as basketball. Cool down by walking or using the trainer.

Friday: Rest.

Saturday: Do any aerobic activity for 45 minutes. If the weather allows, ride outside. Finish with 15 minutes of resistance exercises.

Sunday: If the weather stays nice, ride for 2 hours at a moderate pace. In poor weather, combine activities. For instance, run for 30 minutes, do aerobics for 30 more, ride on the trainer for 45, then stretch and cool down for the remaining 15.

As the weather improves and the days get longer, devote more time during each weekday workout to cycling, and start adding miles to your Sunday ride. You'll be whole-body fit come the heart of the cycling season.

PART FOUR

Body Care

17

What to Do about Saddle Sores

The all-purpose term *saddle sore* includes not only small pimplelike lesions but also chafing, bruises, ulcerated skin, and full-fledged boils. These things have transformed pleasant rides into medieval torture ever since the days of wool shorts with leather chamois. Old-time racers thus afflicted would line their shorts with thin pieces of raw steak to help minimize the pain.

New cyclists are prone to saddle discomforts such as chafing and bruising, although they usually aren't riding enough to run into problems with lesions. A key to dealing with general soreness is to have a good riding position (see chapters 4 and 5), plus a good seat (see "Say No to Numbness" on page 79). After that, regular riding helps to toughen the sitting area. This is often referred to as saddle time, and it's something that every rider needs in order to get more comfortable on the bike.

In the event of broken skin or lesions, a more aggressive approach is needed. Left untreated, saddle sores can become infected and require extended time off the bike. But you don't have to suffer perineal misery (or ruin a good sirloin) if you practice a few simple preventive measures.

Dress for comfort. It's doubtful that you'll still find cycling shorts with a real leather chamois when you go shopping. If you do, don't buy them. Several washings will rob the leather of its natural oils and make perching on its crinkly folds as comfortable as sitting on a tortilla chip. Instead, purchase a high-quality pair of form-fitting spandex shorts with a padded, synthetic liner (still often called a chamois). Modern synthetics are softer on the skin than leather, and they wick moisture that could hasten the formation of sores—something that their animal-based predecessors can't do.

Well-made shorts have a chamois sewn flat so the seams can't rub you raw. Make sure it's large enough to cover your full sitting area. Some liners are one piece while others are stitched from two or three pieces. Most men can be comfortable in any style, but women should go for a one-piece or a curved "baseball" cut that eliminates seams on the midline.

Lubricate yourself. Because friction is a major cause of saddle sores, lubricate your crotch and even the chamois itself with a product made for the purpose, such as Chamois Butt'r. You want something that protects for the duration of rides, but avoid heavy lubes such as petroleum jelly. It can clog your pores and is difficult to wash out of the chamois.

Stay clean. The nasty bacteria that cause boils love hot, moist environments—and nothing is quite as steamy as your hardworking buns, encased in tight-fitting black shorts on a hot summer day. Use an antibacterial soap and water on a washcloth to cleanse your crotch before each ride, especially if you discover that you're prone to sores. Afterward, scrub carefully in the shower and towel dry. Some riders then apply alcohol as a disinfectant, but this can be painful if the skin has been the least bit abraded. It also could dry the skin too much, causing irritation.

Always wear clean cycling shorts for each ride, even on a tour or bike camping trip where washing them may be difficult. Soiled shorts have more bacteria, of course, and they don't breathe as well as freshly laundered ones. Also, don't hang around after a ride with a clammy chamois stuck to your skin. Wash up and change into loose shorts that allow the air to circulate. At night, you can keep your crotch dry for hours at a time by sleeping in the buff.

Turn to medications. If you are prone to saddle sores, *Bicycling* magazine's Fitness Advisory Board member Bernard Burton, M.D., recommends applying a prescription antibiotic gel such as erythromycin after every ride. On a PAC Tour, a 3,200-mile transcontinental ride done in 3 weeks, two cyclists used erythromycin religiously. Result? Not one saddle sore despite averaging 140 miles a day on bumpy back roads.

If you develop a raw area from friction, Dr. Burton recommends an over-the-counter product called Bag Balm, "developed to soothe a milk cow's irritated teats." Look for it at your pharmacy or veterinary store, and cow those saddle sores into submission. "Bag Balm applied to irritated areas after your shower will usually clear up the problem overnight," says Dr. Burton.

Stay on the level. Poor riding position can cause a bumper crop of sores. If your saddle is too high, you'll rock side to side across it as you reach for the pedals, irritating or even breaking your skin. The same can happen when the saddle isn't level. Tilted up, the nose rubs directly on the front of your pubic area as you lean toward the handlebar. Tilted down more than a degree or two, you'll continually slide forward, then

Say No to Numbness

Many cyclists experience periods of genital numbness, which is caused by saddle pressure on the two pudendal nerves in the crotch. This is usually transitory, like a foot falling asleep, but it should still be avoided as much as possible. Otherwise, more serious problems, such as erection difficulties in men, could develop.

Use this checklist to solve genital numbness. By doing so, you'll also be taking steps to reduce the risk of saddle sores.

☐ Is the saddle too far from the handlebar? If you need to lean forward excessively to reach the bar, it makes the nose of the saddle press on the nerves. Install a shorter stem, or move the saddle forward if it won't adversely affect your pedaling position.

☐ Is the nose of the saddle tipped up or down? If it's tipped up, it increases pressure as you lean forward. If it's down, you'll slide onto the narrow nose. Level the saddle by laying a yardstick along its length so that you can compare it to a tabletop, windowsill, or something else horizontal.

☐ Is the saddle too high? This will cause you to saw your crotch side to side in order to reach the pedals. Lower the saddle until you can pedal backward smoothly using your heels.

☐ Is the saddle wide enough for sufficient support? The rear portion must support your ischial tuberosities ("sit bones") to keep pressure off the tender tissue between them. A saddle that's too narrow or domed (when viewed from the rear) puts your sit bones over the sides instead of on top.

☐ Is the saddle too soft? A seat covered by a thick foam or gel padding isn't the solution to numbness. Instead, it actually exerts more pressure on your crotch as your sit bones sink in. Some padding is necessary for comfort, but too much is counterproductive.

☐ Is the saddle up-to-date? A number of recently designed seats have features that reduce the risk of genital numbness, including wedges or holes that remove material where it would contact the crotch. Some models are made specifically for men, others for women. If you decide your present seat should be replaced, check into these anatomical models.

☐ Are you standing enough? During a long ride, periodically pedal out of the saddle for a minute to relieve pressure and restore circulation. This is particularly important if there aren't hills that make standing necessary or if you use an aero bar. It's common to lock into a low, forward position for minutes on end before realizing that numbness is setting in.

push yourself back. The resulting friction can rub you raw. If you suspect that poor position is contributing, check yourself with the pointers in chapters 4 and 5.

Be sure your saddle is wide enough so that your weight is supported on your "sit bones" (ischial tuberosities) rather than by the tender tissue between them. Beware of saddles that have a domed top or lots of foam or gel padding. These conditions cause your sit bones either to be lower on the sides or to sink in. In either case, the center of the saddle presses harder into your crotch.

Take some time off. You don't want to stop riding, but getting the pressure off a budding sore for a couple of days may save you a week or more on the disabled list by preventing it from becoming infected. "Continuing to ride on an abscess," cautions Dr. Burton, "could result in multiple infections, scarring, and the tendency for more of these lesions to develop, even without additional trauma."

Turn on the heat. "Soak in a comfortably hot bathtub three times a day for 15 minutes to allow boils to come to the surface and drain," advises Arnie Baker, M.D., a masters racer and member of *Bicycling* magazine's Fitness Advisory Board. "Hot water increases blood circulation, allowing more of the body's healing factors access to the afflicted area."

Lessen a bumpy ride. In Dr. Burton's estimation, "Riding a bike with rear suspension eliminates about 90 percent of saddle sores. Suspension seatposts also help. Suspension reduces friction because you stay in the seat rather than bouncing up and down on rough ground or pavement."

Emergency Repair

You've obeyed all of the above advice but still sprouted a saddle sore—and the big ride you've planned for all year starts tomorrow. What to do?

Andrew Pruitt, Ed.D., who has served as the medical coordinator for the U.S. national cycling team, suggests applying topical xylocaine and padding the sore with a nonstick moist burn pad such as Spenco Second Skin. This will numb the sore for a few hours of riding.

In many cases, however, cycling is out of the question. Some boils must be lanced and the unfortunate rider given a course of antibiotics. Sometimes, even more heroic measures are required. "When I had bad saddle sores, I continued training," reveals Dr. Baker. "But what I did was hill sprints and intervals—all off the saddle and off my sores."

18

Solve Common Ailments

Cyclists, like most active athletes who work out regularly, can experience a variety of discomforts. Most are minor, but they can still be a nuisance, especially if allowed to go untreated. This handy guide will help you pinpoint your problem and then select the proper remedy.

Ankles

AILMENT: Tenderness at the back of your ankle (Achilles tendinitis)

CAUSES:

- Inadequate warmup

- Climbing in too high a gear

- Improper saddle height or cleat position

SOLUTIONS:

- Stretch before riding; start rides by spinning easily in low gears.

- Use lower gears for climbing; alternate sitting and standing.

- Raise the saddle slightly; be sure the cleat position doesn't place the ball of your foot behind the pedal axle.

Buttocks (glutes)

AILMENTS: Discomfort, chafing, saddle sores

CAUSES:

- Too little or too much saddle time

- A seat that's too narrow, wide, or hard

- Improper riding apparel

- Poor hygiene

SOLUTIONS:

- Ride regularly to condition yourself to the saddle, but don't increase mileage by more than 10 percent per week.

- Use a moderately padded saddle that supports you on your "sit bones" (ischial tuberosities) but isn't so soft or wide that it causes chafing.

- Wear cycling shorts with a soft, absorbent liner (chamois).

- Wash your crotch before and after every ride; apply a skin lube such as Chamois Butt'r before every ride; wash your shorts after every ride.

Eyes

AILMENTS: Fatigue, dryness
CAUSES:
- Overexposure to ultraviolet (UV) radiation

- Wind penetration; poor tearing
SOLUTIONS:
- Wear sunglasses with shatterproof lenses that block 100 percent of UV radiation.

- Wear wraparound-style sunglasses; use a wetting solution.

Feet

AILMENT: A burning sensation or numbness in the ball of your foot
CAUSES:
- Tight shoes

- Hard plastic soles

- Tight laces or straps

- Improper cleat position
SOLUTIONS:
- Wear cycling shoes large enough to accommodate the slight swelling that occurs on longer rides.

- Install a thin cushion insole.

- Loosen laces or straps at the first sign of foot discomfort.

- Move cleats rearward so that the ball of your foot is slightly in front of the pedal axle, reducing pressure.

Hands

AILMENT: Numbness and loss of grip strength (ulnar neuropathy)
CAUSE:
- Excessive hand pressure on the handlebar

SOLUTIONS:

■ Wear cycling gloves with padded palms.

■ Install padded handlebar tape or softer grips.

■ Change hand positions frequently while riding.

Hips

AILMENTS: Chronic soreness, contusions

CAUSES:

■ Improper saddle height or leg-length discrepancy

■ Pushing big gears

■ Crashing

SOLUTIONS:

■ Adjust the saddle height so your hips don't have to rock side to side to help you reach the pedals; put a shim between the cleat and shoe of the shorter leg, or have a podiatrist design an orthotic (a shoe insert).

■ Use gears no larger than you can spin at about 90 rpm.

■ Apply ice periodically until swelling subsides, then resume easy riding to loosen the area and encourage bloodflow.

Knees

AILMENTS: Stiffness, soreness, pain

CAUSES:

■ Pushing too big a gear

■ Increasing mileage too rapidly

■ Improper cleat position

■ Incorrect saddle height

■ Insufficient clothing

SOLUTIONS:

■ Use gears no larger than you can spin at about 90 rpm.

■ Increase mileage and intensity no more than 10 percent per week.

■ Position cleats to accommodate the natural angle of your feet or use a pedal system that allows your feet to "float" to their natural position.

- Position the saddle so that each knee remains slightly bent at the bottom of the pedal stroke. If the pain is behind your knee, lower the saddle; if in front, raise the saddle.

- Ride in tights or leg warmers when the temperature is below 65°F.

Lower Back

AILMENTS: Stiffness, soreness, pain

CAUSES:

- Leaning over the handlebar for extended periods

- Handlebar too low in relation to saddle

- Overly long reach to the handlebar

- Leg-length discrepancy

SOLUTIONS:

- Stretch before every ride; vary your riding position by changing hand location and standing regularly; do crunches to strengthen the stomach muscles that support your lower back.

- Raise the handlebar to within an inch of the seat height.

- Install a handlebar stem with less extension. When you're riding with your hands on the brake lever hoods, your view of the front hub should be blocked by the handlebar.

- Put a shim between the cleat and shoe of the shorter leg, or have a podiatrist design an orthotic (a shoe insert).

Neck

AILMENTS: Stiffness, pain

CAUSES:

- Heavy helmet

- Stationary head position

- Riding position too low

SOLUTIONS:

- Wear a lighter helmet that still meets safety standards.

- Periodically tilt your head from side to side while riding.

- Raise the handlebar or install a stem with a shorter extension.

Shoulders

AILMENTS: Stiffness, soreness

CAUSES:

■ Riding with locked elbows

■ Improper handlebar width

■ Improper handlebar stem extension or height

SOLUTIONS:

■ Keep your elbows bent and relaxed to absorb shock.

■ Install a handlebar that equals your shoulder width.

■ Raise the handlebar to within an inch of seat height; install a stem with the proper extension. When riding with your hands on the brake lever hoods, your view of the front hub should be blocked by the handlebar.

Skin

AILMENTS: Sunburn, skin cancer, abrasions

CAUSES:

■ Overexposure to ultraviolet (UV) radiation

■ Crashing

SOLUTIONS:

■ Use sunscreen with an SPF of at least 15; cover burned areas with clothing to prevent further damage.

■ See a doctor about suspicious lesions or moles.

■ Clean wound thoroughly and cover with an antibiotic salve and breathable dressing, which should be changed each morning and evening.

Thighs (quadriceps)

AILMENTS: Soreness, cramps

CAUSES:

■ Exceptionally hard or prolonged riding

■ Inadequate training

■ Insufficient fluid replacement

SOLUTIONS:

■ Spin easily for recovery; massage.

■ Gradually increase intensity during the season; don't increase mileage by more than 10 percent per week.

■ Drink at least one bottle of liquid per hour (more in hot weather) and use sports drinks that contain electrolytes, which combat cramping.

19
Ask the Fitness Experts

Bicycling magazine's editors and members of its Fitness Advisory Board receive lots of medical and fitness questions each month from its readers. Here's a selection that addresses several concerns that you may have as a new cyclist.

Knee Pain

Q: *When pedaling hard—uphill, against the wind, or in big gears— why do I get a grinding sensation and pain in the front of my knee?*

A: This is chondromalacia, the most common knee complaint. It's an irritation or roughness behind the kneecap. Cycling is actually beneficial for most sufferers, if done properly.

There are two key factors: saddle height and cadence. If you have chondromalacia, your saddle should be as high as you can tolerate without your hips rocking or your knee overextending when the pedal is at its lowest position. And your cadence should be above 90 rpm. That is, each foot should come around the pedal circle at least 90 times per minute. Count the number of revolutions your right foot makes in 30 seconds, then multiply by two. This combination will keep your kneecap from being overstressed.

In your noncycling activities, avoid squatting, kneeling, and climbing stairs. Ice the knee after riding and strengthen your medial thigh muscles with short-arc knee extensions. Here's how.

Sit on the floor, your legs straight out in front of you, with two bath towels rolled up together and placed under your knee. Wear up to 10 pounds of ankle weights. Slowly straighten the knee and hold for a second. Do 100 repetitions per knee each day. This will strengthen the vastus medialis muscle of the quadriceps, which positions and stabilizes the kneecap.

This exercise can't be done correctly on knee-extension machines that cause the knee to move through a full 90-degree arc.

Endurance Food

Q: *What can I eat and drink to improve endurance?*

A: The most important consideration is the amount of carbohydrate because it's the best and most efficient fuel for riding. Simple carbohydrate is a single or double sugar molecule and is found in fruit as well as candy. Complex carbohydrate is a long chain of simple sugars and is often called a starch. It's found in such foods as potatoes and pasta. Simple and complex carbos are equally effective at providing energy for a hard effort. But complex carbo is superior in that it provides vitamins, minerals, and fiber along with the energy.

When you consume carbohydrate, it's broken down and converted to blood glucose, which is used as fuel or energy. If it's not immediately needed, it gets stored in your muscles and liver as glycogen. To build your glycogen stores, eat whole-grain breads, cereals, pasta, and potatoes. On the bike, good choices include fruits and energy bars. The latter has more carbohydrate than an apple or banana.

To be physiologically effective, an energy drink should contain 6 to 10 percent carbohydrate in addition to its supply of sodium, potassium, and other nutrients. Most have the correct percentage when mixed as the label directs. You may want to avoid drinks high in fructose, which can cause stomach upset or diarrhea in some people. If fructose is listed first on the ingredient label, be wary.

But exactly what you should eat and drink is a matter of personal choice. In general, avoid high-fat items and choose foods and drinks that taste good. If you don't like the way something tastes, it doesn't matter how much quick energy it packs, you won't eat it. Experiment on your training rides. Your sense of taste is different on the bike than when you're at rest.

Leg Shaving

Q: *Why do guys shave their legs? Does it improve performance?*

A: It's traditional in cycling for men (and women) to shave. First, it makes it easier to clean and bandage abrasions because hair can't get caught in the wound. Second, hairless legs are easier to massage—an excellent form of relaxation and recovery after hard rides. Third, wind tunnel tests have actually proven that shaved legs save a bit of time (about 5 seconds in a 25-mile time trial). Plus, they're marginally cooler on hot days. But perhaps the best reason for recreational riders is an aesthetic one: You look a lot better without hairy legs sticking out of tight spandex cycling shorts, and shaving shows off leg muscles a lot more impressively.

Thigh Size

Q: *Some pro cyclists have very muscular legs, while others have thin, gangly ones. What can I do to make sure mine become the bigger and stronger type?*

A: There's definitely a difference in the way some cyclists' muscles respond to training. It depends on the type of muscle fiber you have—slow twitch or fast twitch. Cyclists with a high proportion of fast-twitch fibers will experience a greater increase in muscle size and strength with training. Cyclists with a high proportion of slow-twitch fibers won't see much change in size but will excel in endurance.

Riders with muscular thighs are usually exceptionally good at sprints and short hills. Thin-thighed cyclists tend to be better at steady distance riding. Of course, there are always exceptions.

Muscle fiber type is genetically determined and can't be changed. If you want to develop thigh strength, do a lot of hill climbing, sprint work, and leg presses or squats. If you don't respond particularly well, then you probably don't have a high percentage of fast-twitch fibers. But consistent cycling will give definition to your leg muscles even if it doesn't pump up their size very much.

Riding with a Cold

Q: *Is it okay to keep cycling when I catch a cold?*

A: Cycling coaches have always said that training is fine if no fever or lung congestion is present. Recent studies have found, however, that muscles can be damaged by exercising when an infection is present. Even worse, viruses that produce upper-respiratory infections can also attack the heart muscle, a potentially life-threatening condition. So the next time a cold strikes, it may be smart to rest instead of riding, at least until it's nearly gone. Easy riding can then help clear congestion.

Cycling during Menstruation

Q: *Is it okay for a woman to ride during her period?*

A: Women were once urged to avoid exercising (and even to avoid polite company) during "certain times of the month." But science does not support this warning. For example, the production of lactic acid (a substance in the muscles that inhibits performance) is no greater during menstruation, and we know that women—including cyclists—have set records and won Olympic medals during all phases of their menstrual cycles.

Still, many women feel tired or less enthusiastic about their workouts at specific times each month. Such fatigue or malaise varies widely from woman to woman, and science can't readily account for it. For those who experience it, doctors usually recommend charting cycles for several months and noting those times when you're least inspired to exercise. Then, simply plan to train lightly or rest on those days.

If menstrual cramping interferes with their cycling, many women find that the nonprescription drug ibuprofen helps so well that they can exercise without difficulty shortly after taking the recommended dosage.

While menstruation should have little effect on your cycling, there is debate as to what cycling can do to menstruation. Some doctors have claimed that strenuous training will disrupt a woman's cycle, interfering with her fertility and possibly her health. In certain cases, women athletes have stopped having their periods, a condition known as amenorrhea. This won't permanently affect the ability to become pregnant, but amenorrhea may influence how the body stores calcium. No period means little or no estrogen production, and estrogen is essential for calcium storage. Consequently, amenorrheic women are thought to be at greater risk of developing osteoporosis.

It's interesting to note that in most studies, the athletes who developed menstrual irregularities were serious runners. Few cyclists had problems. But if your period does change, either after you begin riding regularly or after you increase your mileage, see a doctor—preferably a gynecologist who is familiar with athletic amenorrhea.

Energy Use

Q: *How many calories does cycling burn?*

A: There's no precise answer because there are so many factors (body size, type of bike, terrain, and wind conditions). But it is known that the energy used in cycling varies dramatically as speed changes, thanks to wind resistance. "Calorie Consumption" shows estimates for different weights and speeds. These numbers were developed by physiologist James Hagberg, Ph.D. Simply choose your average speed, multiply your body weight by the coefficient for that speed, and you'll find the approximate number of calories you burn per minute.

Going uphill adds to this energy cost. According to *Bicycling* magazine's Fitness Advisory Board member David Swain, Ph.D., it takes an additional 22 calories for every 100 feet of elevation gained. (This is an average value for a cyclist and bike weighing a total of 176 pounds.) Coasting downhill burns no calories, of course, but the combination of going up and then down always uses more energy than traveling on flat ground.

Calorie Consumption

AVG SPEED (MPH)	COEFFICIENT (CAL/LB/MIN)
8	0.0295
10	0.0355
12	0.0426
14	0.0512
15	0.0561
16	0.0615
17	0.0675
18	0.0740
19	0.0811
20	0.0891
21	0.0975
23	0.1173
25	0.1411

PART FIVE

Bicycle Care

20
Fix Flats Fast

Sooner or later, it will happen. You'll be pedaling along when you hear hissing or a sudden kapow, and one end of the bike will sink. Yep, it's a flat tire, the most common breakdown you'll face as a cyclist. Worry not; repairing flats is simple.

Here's a step-by-step tube-replacement guide. Make a copy to keep in your seatbag with your repair kit. You won't need instructions after you've done the procedure a few times.

Because patching tires with highway tar is virtually impossible, fast flat fixing starts with having the right supplies. Your underseat bag should include the following:

- A spare tube of the correct size
- Two tire levers
- A patch kit (for the inevitable second puncture)
- A pump or CO_2 cartridge
- Enough change to call for help if you suffer a blowout that can't be repaired

Make sure your spare tube and inflation device match your valve type, either Schrader (as found on auto tires) or presta (the narrow European style).

The procedure below is for a rear flat because rear-wheel removal is more complicated than front-wheel removal. Actual tube replacement is the same for both wheels.

Remove the Wheel and Tube

1. Before rolling to a stop, shift to the smallest cog. If you don't have time, pedal by hand and shift after you get off. This moves the derailleur as far from under the wheel as possible. If there's a peg on the inside of the right seatstay, lift the chain onto it with a tire lever or your finger.

2. Spread the brake pads by whatever means provided, which may be unhooking a cable or using a quick-release on the brake or its lever. Open the hub quick-release by pivoting its lever.

3. To remove the wheel, lift the bike by the seat with one hand while pushing the wheel forward and down with the other. If the chain clings to the cogs, shake the wheel to free it. Once the wheel is out, lay the bike on its left side so that the drivetrain isn't on the ground.

4. Remove the valve cap and deflate the tube completely by depressing the spring-loaded center pin on a Schrader valve or by unscrewing and depressing the pin on a presta valve.

5. Insert the flat, spoonlike end of one tire lever between the tire bead and the rim about 2 inches from the valve. Lift up the bead by pulling the lever down and hooking it to a spoke.

6. Insert the second lever under the same bead about 4 inches farther from the valve. Pull the lever down, prying off more of the bead (see photo). You should now be able to slide the second lever along the rim to free the entire side of the tire. If the bead is too tight, hold the dislodged portion with your hand and move several inches farther along with the second lever. You don't need to unseat the other bead from the rim.

7. Starting opposite the valve, pull the inner tube from the tire. Then pull out the valve stem.

Use tire levers to dislodge the bead on one side.

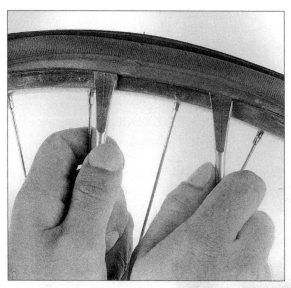

Find the Puncture

1. Locate the puncture by inflating the tube and listening for a hiss. Water or saliva rubbed on a leak will bubble to confirm you've found the right spot.

2. Hold the valve stem next to the rim's valve hole so you can match the hole in the tube to the tire. Look closely at the tread and casing to find the hole or cut. You might see a shard of glass or other sharp object lodged in the tread. Pick it out, then double-check by carefully feeling around the inside of the tire.

3. If the tire has a hole larger than ⅛ inch or a cut in the sidewall, you must cover it, or the new tube will squeeze through and blow out. Use an appropriate size patch from your repair kit. If you've left your kit at home, roam the roadside for a tough piece of paper or use a folded dollar bill (it's made of linen). Place the material across the hole as you install the spare tube. Inflate only to 75 percent of maximum pressure and you should be able to ride home safely.

Install the Spare Tube

1. Inflate the spare tube just enough to unflatten it.

2. Insert the valve stem through the rim.

3. Carefully tuck the entire tube into the tire so that there are no kinks or wrinkles.

4. Begin working the tire onto the rim, starting at the valve. Use your hands instead of tire levers so you don't accidentally cause another puncture by pinching the tube.

The last section may become tight and hard to get onto the rim. Deflate the tube completely to minimize its size, then use your thumbs or palms to force the tire into place.

5. Push the valve stem into the tire to ensure that the tube isn't trapped under the bead, then pull it down firmly.

6. Inflate to about half the pressure listed on the tire sidewall. Hold the hub axle in your hands so that you can spin the wheel and watch the bead line molded into each side of the tire. It should appear just above the rim. If it bulges up, let out the air and work that section with your hands to get the tube out from under the bead. If it dips below, continue inflating to maximum recommended pressure, and you'll probably hear it pop into place. Spin the wheel, and eye the line again to make sure. Rub a little saliva or soap on a section of tire that refuses to seat under full pressure.

Install the Wheel

1. Hold the bike upright by the seat or left seatstay with your left hand. Roll the wheel into place.

2. Use your right hand to pull back the rear derailleur. Set the top run of chain onto the smallest cog (the position the drivetrain was in before you removed the wheel). Set the bike down so that the axle is positioned in front of the dropouts, then pull the wheel back into the slots.

3. Make sure the wheel is centered in the frame. A good indicator is equal distance between the tire and chainstays behind the bottom bracket.

4. Close the hub quick-release. The lever should require enough force to make an imprint on your palm. If necessary, turn the nut on the other end until the lever tightens firmly enough.

5. Close the brake release. Make sure the wheel spins without rubbing.

6. Pick up all of your gear and stow it in your seatbag or pockets.

Patch the Tube

On the road, it's easier and quicker to install a spare tube than to patch the punctured one. Carry the bad boy home and patch it later for use as a spare. Here's how.

1. Choose the right patch. Small round ones are for pinhole punctures, while oval patches fit the dual "snakebite" holes made by a rim pinch. Blowouts cause a large hole that usually can't be reliably patched.

2. Locate the puncture by putting air in the tube, then running it past your ear or lips to hear or feel the spot where air is escaping. Still can't find it? Put a section at a time in a sink full of water until you see the telltale bubbles. Once you find the hole, draw an X across it with a ballpoint pen. This will stay visible during the repair.

3. Buff the area with sandpaper. This rough section needs to be a bit larger than the patch.

4. Apply a thin, even coat of glue to the buffed surface and give it a couple of minutes to dry. It will turn from shiny to dull.

5. Peel the backing from the patch and apply it carefully to the glued area, pressing it firmly in place (you get only one chance). Some patches have foil on one side and cellophane on the other. The surface under the foil goes against the glue. Leave the cellophane on so that the patch won't stick to the inside of the tire.

21
Quick Mountain Bike Tune-Up

Though touted as indestructible, mountain bikes do need occasional tune-ups. In fact, if they're ridden regularly or aggressively off-road, they'll need the following service every month or two. The mud, crud, and sludge found in the outback can foul things quickly. If you keep your bike clean, lubed, and adjusted according to these instructions, it will ride better and last longer.

Note: This quick tune-up isn't appropriate for a thrashed bike. If your rig has gone for a year without service, if the wheels are bent, if the cables and housings are frayed or cracked, or if the chain is frozen with rust, you should take the bike to a good shop for an overhaul. Once everything is back in order, use this tune-up procedure to keep it that way.

1. Wash the bike. Fill a bucket with warm soapy water. Put the bike in a repair stand outside or spread newspapers beneath it. Shift to the largest chainring and middle cog. Coat the chain with degreaser and let

Tools and Supplies

☐ Bucket	☐ Small regular screwdriver
☐ Detergent	☐ Lube
☐ Repair stand	☐ Pump
☐ Newspapers	☐ Grease
☐ Degreaser	☐ Spoke wrench
☐ Toothbrush	☐ Acetone
☐ Sponges	☐ 4-, 5-, 6-, and 8-mm allen wrenches
☐ Brushes	☐ Pedal wrench
☐ Rags	☐ Brake pads (about $4 each)

it sit for 10 minutes. Then scrub it clean by hand-pedaling the bike while squeezing the sponge around the chain. Now shift to the smallest ring/smallest cog combination. Spread the brake pads by using each brake's quick-release or by unhooking the crossover cable. Open the hub quick-releases and remove the wheels. Refill the bucket. Scrub the bike and wheels with a clean sponge and brushes.

2. Apply degreaser to the chainrings and cogs. Use the toothbrush to clean the chainrings (see photo). If dirt or grass is stuffed between the cogs, dig it out with a small screwdriver. When you wash the wheels, pay special attention to the tire sidewalls. Look for cuts or fraying threads that indicate that the tire should be replaced. To rinse the bike, drip water on the frame and wheels from above. Then dry the frame, components, and wheels with clean rags. Finally, lube the chain.

3. Check the headset and lube the cables. Most modern mountain bikes have threadless headsets, which are easier to service than conventional types. Check yours by standing in front of the bike, grabbing the fork, and pushing and pulling. If there's any play, loosen the stem binder bolts, turn the screw atop the stem clockwise just enough to eliminate play, and tighten the stem bolts. If this doesn't work, have the adjustment checked by a shop mechanic. If there are bare cable sections, re-lube the cables by releasing the housing ends from the stops. If the ends are stuck, push them out with a screwdriver. For the rear brake, pull on the housing and lift it out of the stops. Free the other housing section similarly. Then slide them aside and lube the newly exposed portion of cable. For derailleur cables, push the derailleur inward to create slack. Then lift the housing out of the frame stops, slide it down the cable, and lube the exposed section. If you can't release the housings, your cables are probably sealed and don't need lubing.

4. Inflate the tires and reinstall the wheels. Make sure they're fully inserted and centered in the frame and that the hub quick-releases are tight. Check for loose spokes. Start at the valve stem and wiggle each one. Keep in mind that the left-side spokes on the rear wheel are looser than the other three sets. Compare them only to each other. If you find loose spokes, tighten them by turning the nipples in half-turn increments until they're as tight as adjacent ones. Then spin the wheels to gauge trueness. Hold your thumb against a brake or the frame and watch the gap between your thumb and the rim. To move the rim to the right, loosen the left nipples and tighten the right ones. Proceed in half-turn increments (when viewed from outside the rim) until the wobble is gone. Repeat until the wheels are true. Clean the rims with acetone to remove brake-pad deposits.

5. Tighten everything. Major components can loosen from the rigors of trail riding. So check everything with the appropriate wrenches. Don't force, but try to tighten both crankarm bolts, the pedals (remember the left one tightens counterclockwise), chainring bolts (don't forget those behind the small ring), stem binder, handlebar binder, bar-end binders, seat binder, seat bolt, brake and derailleur nuts and bolts, brake- and shift-lever bolts, and water bottle and rack screws.

6. Remove, clean, and test your frame pump. If it isn't pumping, try unscrewing the top, extracting the rod, and adding grease to the plunger. Check your patch kit. Do you still have patches? Has the glue evaporated? Lube the pivot points of clipless pedals, front and rear derailleurs, and brakes.

7. Check derailleur adjustments. Shift through all the gear combinations. Hesitation when shifting to larger cogs is a sign that the cable has stretched. To speed shifts, turn the adjusting barrel on the back of the derailleur counterclockwise a half-turn and recheck. Repeat until

Clean the chainrings with a toothbrush.

the derailleur shifts to the next cog with each click of the lever. If shifts to larger chainrings aren't crisp, perform the same fix for the front derailleur by turning the adjusting barrel on the shift lever.

8. Check brake pads. These are the parts that wear quickest on mountain bikes, especially if you're a mud monster. Check the surface of each pad. There should be grooves. If not, the pads are worn and should be replaced. To do this, look for adjusting barrels on the brake levers and thread them in fully. (You might have to loosen a locknut first.) Then replace the pads individually. Copy the position of the opposite pad as closely as possible, and tighten the locknut to secure it. To check the position, push the brake arm in, and note how the pad strikes the rim. It should hit squarely but be angled just a tad so that the front tip touches first. This is called toe-in and will prevent squealing. Hook up the crossover cable and squeeze the brake levers to check the feel. If you like less lever play, unscrew the adjustment barrels slightly and hold their position with the locknut (if available).

9. Service the suspension. If you have suspension on your bike— front, rear, or both—read your owner's manual to see what service is required. For instance, the pressure should be checked regularly on air shocks, and elastomer forks should be disassembled, cleaned, and lubed. The pivots on dual-suspension frames can loosen and should be secured or lubed. If you don't have the owner's manual, contact a local shop for advice or call the company that built your bike or shock.

22
Rapid Road Bike Tune-Up

It's Saturday night. The club century is tomorrow. You're carbo-loaded, superhydrated, and ready to hit the hay early. But is your bike ready?

Even new or just-repaired machines should be checked before every major event, preferably with enough time for a thorough test ride. It's the only way to catch the small problems that can lead to breakdowns or even accidents.

This routine tune-up should take about an hour. Once you have the tools, it's manageable by the average home mechanic. Besides finding and fixing glitches before a big ride, it'll boost your confidence that you

Tools and Supplies

- ☐ Repair stand
- ☐ Spray cleaner/polish
- ☐ Rags
- ☐ Long screwdriver
- ☐ Degreaser
- ☐ Bucket
- ☐ Detergent
- ☐ Sponges
- ☐ Headset wrenches
- ☐ 4-, 5-, and 6-mm allen wrenches
- ☐ Awl
- ☐ Pump
- ☐ Spoke wrench
- ☐ Crank bolt wrench
- ☐ Pedal wrench
- ☐ 10-mm combination wrench
- ☐ Grease
- ☐ Lube
- ☐ Brake pads

can handle almost anything that goes wrong with your bike. Keep in mind that this procedure works only on reasonably maintained bikes in good condition. Bikes in bad shape may need a complete overhaul (including repacking bearings).

1. Clean the bike. Place it in a repair stand (outside if possible). If it's only slightly dirty, apply a spray cleaner/polish made for bicycles to the frame and parts, then wipe with a clean rag. For a filthy bike, remove both wheels and put a long screwdriver through the triangular hole in the rear dropouts to hold up the chain. Spray the chain and derailleurs with degreaser and let the bike sit for a few minutes. Fill the bucket with warm soapy water. Douse an old sponge, hold it on the chain, and turn the crankset to draw the chain through until the links sparkle. Clean the crankset and derailleurs as well. Then wash the frame and parts (including wheels) with a fresh sponge. When everything is clean, rinse by dribbling water from above. (Don't spray directly at the bike, because this can force water into the bearings.) Dry the bike and parts with clean rags.

2. Check the bearings. Stand in front of the bike, holding the fork in one hand and the down tube in the other. Push and pull on the fork to check for play in the headset bearings. Turn the fork slowly from side to side to feel for roughness. If it's loose or tight, adjust nut-style headsets by loosening the top nut with a headset wrench or large adjustable wrench, then slightly tighten or loosen the cone (underneath the top nut) with another. Next, tighten the top nut against the cone while you hold it in place. For threadless headsets, loosen the stem binder bolts, then remove play or tightness by adjusting the allen screw atop the stem, and finish by securing the stem bolts. Now check the bottom bracket bearings. Stand beside the frame, hold the crankarms, and push and pull, feeling for play. Most modern bottom brackets are sealed and reliable. If yours is loose, have a shop remove the crankarms and adjust it. Finally, check the hub bearings. If the wheels are in the frame, grasp each rim and wiggle it laterally to feel for looseness. If the wheels are out, remove the quick-release skewers and turn and wiggle each axle with your fingers. A hint of looseness is okay. Should there be more than that, or if there is binding, take the wheels to your shop for service.

3. Inspect the tires. Look for sidewall cracks, tread cuts, bald tread, and so on. Replace tires if you find such damage or wear. Search for objects embedded in the tread. Pick them out with an awl before they can work their way through and cause a puncture. Also, check tire seating. There are molded lines on the base of the sidewalls that should sit just above the rim all the way around. If they dip below the rim edge or rise above it, the tire will roll poorly and possibly blow off. If you find either problem, deflate the tire, massage the area, then inflate it, watching to be sure it seats correctly. Inflate both tires to the pressure marked on the sidewall. Install the wheels on the bike, making sure that they're centered in the frame.

4. True the wheels. Starting at the valve stem, work your way around each wheel, grabbing and wiggling spokes to see if any are loose. After a few spokes you'll get a feel for correct tension. Keep in mind that the left-side spokes on the rear wheel are always looser than the others— just make sure they're evenly tensioned compared to each other. If you find a loose spoke, tighten it by turning the nipple counterclockwise (when it's at the bottom of the wheel and you're looking down on it) in half-turn increments until it's tensioned like its neighbors. Then spin the wheels and sight trueness by looking at the gap between the rim and brake pad. True the wheels if necessary. To move the rim to the left, loosen right nipples and tighten left nipples in the problem area. Do the reverse to move it right. Go easy. Always turn nipples a half-turn at a time and check your progress frequently.

5. Snug all parts. Though major components shouldn't loosen with normal use, it's wise to check them with the appropriate wrenches. Without forcing, try to tighten both crank bolts, pedals, chainring bolts (don't forget those behind the little ring if you have triple chainrings),

stem binder, handlebar binder, seat binder, seat bolt, brake and derailleur attaching nuts and bolts, and the bottle cage and rack screws.
(Everything is turned clockwise to tighten except the left pedal, which is
turned counterclockwise.)

6. Remove and test the frame pump. If it doesn't inflate properly,
try unscrewing the top, extracting the rod, and adding grease to the
plunger. Check your patch kit. Does it have patches? Has the glue evaporated? If so, replace it. Finally, put a drop of lube on the pivot points of
clipless pedals, derailleurs, and brakes.

7. Adjust the shifting. Lube the shift cables where they pass the
bottom bracket. Lube the chain, then shift through the gears repeatedly
to test derailleur adjustments. Because the rear derailleur's cable is
longer and gets more use, it's more likely to go out of adjustment. Each
click of the rear shift lever should cause the chain to immediately jump
to the next cog. If not, the cable has probably stretched or you may have
adjusted it too tightly. If the chain hesitates to go to a larger cog, the
cable is slightly loose. If it hesitates to drop to a smaller cog, it's tight.
Fix slow shifts to larger cogs by turning the adjustment barrel on the
rear of the derailleur counterclockwise in half-turn increments. For slow
shifts to smaller cogs, turn the barrel clockwise (see photo).

8. Inspect the brake pads. If the grooves are almost worn away, re-place the pads. Make sure they strike the rim squarely. If they don't, loosen the nut with an allen or 10-mm wrench and reposition them. Squeeze the brake levers to feel the action. The pads should strike the rim well before the levers approach the handlebar. If not, snug the brake cable by turning the barrel on the brake caliper. If it's one piece, turn it counterclockwise until the pads are ⅛ to ¼ inch away from the rim. If the barrel has two pieces, turn the ring on the barrel clockwise to tighten the brake (you might have to lift the barrel to get the ring to turn). If the pads don't release equally, center the brake with the small screw on top (Shimano) or allen on the side (Campagnolo) of the brake arm. On old-style brakes, slightly loosen the attaching nut behind the brake, center the caliper, then tighten the nut. Or, look for flats on the pivot bolt (next to the frame) that allow centering with a brake or cone wrench.

9. Test ride the bike. Shift and brake repeatedly, then fine-tune if necessary. If the brakes squeal, determine which one is making the noise. Toe in the pad by making the front end contact the rim first. Many pads, such as those from Campagnolo, have washers that permit toeing the pad after loosening the nut. Position them to produce a 1-mm gap between the back of the pad and the rim (on contact), then tighten the nut. If the pads don't have toeing hardware, it's possible to adjust them by bending the brake arm with an adjustable wrench. Open the jaws just enough to slide over the arm. Go easy so that you don't break the brake.

Anatomy of a Bike

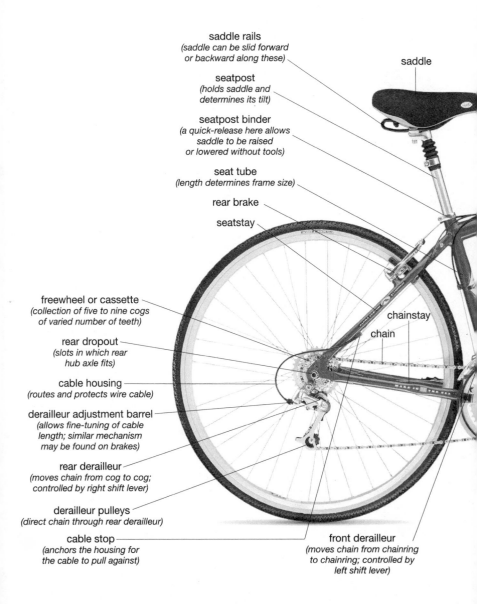

saddle rails
*(saddle can be slid forward
or backward along these)*

saddle

seatpost
*(holds saddle and
determines its tilt)*

seatpost binder
*(a quick-release here allows
saddle to be raised
or lowered without tools)*

seat tube
(length determines frame size)

rear brake

seatstay

freewheel or cassette
*(collection of five to nine cogs
of varied number of teeth)*

chainstay

chain

rear dropout
*(slots in which rear
hub axle fits)*

cable housing
(routes and protects wire cable)

derailleur adjustment barrel
*(allows fine-tuning of cable
length; similar mechanism
may be found on brakes)*

rear derailleur
*(moves chain from cog to cog;
controlled by right shift lever)*

derailleur pulleys
(direct chain through rear derailleur)

cable stop
*(anchors the housing for
the cable to pull against)*

front derailleur
*(moves chain from chainring
to chainring; controlled by
left shift lever)*

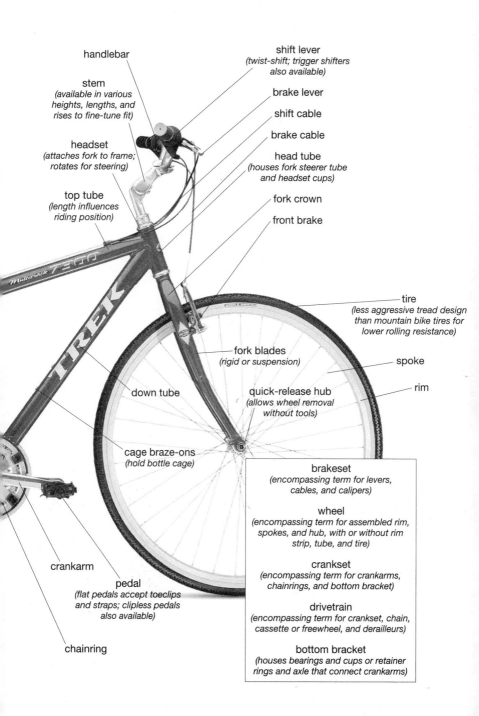

handlebar

shift lever
*(twist-shift; trigger shifters
also available)*

stem
*(available in various
heights, lengths, and
rises to fine-tune fit)*

brake lever

shift cable

brake cable

headset
*(attaches fork to frame;
rotates for steering)*

head tube
*(houses fork steerer tube
and headset cups)*

top tube
*(length influences
riding position)*

fork crown

front brake

tire
*(less aggressive tread design
than mountain bike tires for
lower rolling resistance)*

fork blades
(rigid or suspension)

spoke

down tube

rim

quick-release hub
*(allows wheel removal
without tools)*

cage braze-ons
(hold bottle cage)

brakeset
*(encompassing term for levers,
cables, and calipers)*

wheel
*(encompassing term for assembled rim,
spokes, and hub, with or without rim
strip, tube, and tire)*

crankarm

crankset
*(encompassing term for crankarms,
chainrings, and bottom bracket)*

pedal
*(flat pedals accept toeclips
and straps; clipless pedals
also available)*

drivetrain
*(encompassing term for crankset, chain,
cassette or freewheel, and derailleurs)*

chainring

bottom bracket
*(houses bearings and cups or retainer
rings and axle that connect crankarms)*

Glossary

This glossary will help you learn cycling's many special words and phrases. While not every term is used in this book, you'll hear them all when involved in the sport.

A

Aerobic: Exercise at an intensity that allows the body's need for oxygen to be continually met. This intensity can be sustained for long periods.

Aerodynamic: A design of cycling equipment or a riding position that reduces wind resistance. "Aero" for short.

Anaerobic: Exercise above the intensity at which the body's need for oxygen can be met. This intensity can be sustained only briefly.

Apex: The sharpest part of a turn where the transition from entering to exiting takes place.

B

Bead: In tires, the edge along each side's inner circumference that fits into the rim.

Berm: A small embankment along the edge of a trail, often occurring in turns.

Blood glucose: A sugar, glucose is the only fuel that can be used by the brain.

Blow up: To suddenly be unable to continue at the required pace due to overexertion.

Bonk: A state of severe exhaustion caused mainly by the depletion of glycogen in the muscles because the rider has failed to eat or drink enough. Once it occurs, rest and high-carbohydrate foods are necessary for recovery.

Boot: A small piece of material used inside a tire to cover a cut in the tread or sidewall. Without it, the tube will push through and blow out.

Bottom bracket: The part of the frame where the crankset is installed. Also, the axle, cups, and bearings of the crankset.

BPM: Abbreviation for "beats per minute" in reference to heart rate.

Bunnyhop: A way to ride over obstacles such as rocks or logs, in which both wheels leave the ground.

C

Cadence: The number of times during 1 minute that a pedal stroke is completed. Also called pedal rpm.

Carbohydrate: In the diet, it is broken down into glucose, the body's principal energy source, through digestion and metabolism. It is stored as glycogen in the liver and muscles. Carbo can be simple (sugars) or complex (bread, pasta, grains, fruits, vegetables); the latter type contains additional nutrients. One gram of carbohydrate supplies 4 calories.

Cardiovascular: Pertaining to the heart and blood vessels.

Cassette: The set of gear cogs on the rear hub. Also called a freewheel, cluster, or block.

Catch air: When both wheels leave the ground, usually because of a rise or dip in the riding surface.

Century: A 100-mile ride.

Chainring: A sprocket on the crankset. There may be one, two, or three. The short version is "ring."

Chainsuck: When the chain sticks to the chainring teeth during a downshift and gets drawn up and jammed between the small ring and the frame.

Chondromalacia: A serious knee injury in which there is disintegration of cartilage surfaces due to improper tracking of the kneecap. Symptoms start with deep knee pain and a crunching sensation during bending.

Circuit: A course that is ridden two or more times to compose the race.

Clean: In mountain biking, to ride through a difficult, technical section without putting a foot down (dabbing).

Cleat: A metal or plastic fitting on the sole of a cycling shoe that engages the pedal.

Clincher: A conventional tire with a separate inner tube.

Cog: A sprocket on the rear wheel's cassette or freewheel.

Contact patch: The portion of a tire in touch with the ground.

Crash rash: Any skin abrasion resulting from a fall. Also called road rash.

Cross-training: Combining sports for mental refreshment and physical conditioning, especially during cycling's off-season.

D

Dab: To put a foot on the ground to prevent falling over.

Doubletrack: Two parallel trails formed by the wheel ruts of off-road vehicles. Also called a Jeep trail.

Downshift: To shift to a lower gear, that is, a larger cog or smaller chainring.

Drafting: Riding closely behind another rider to take advantage of the windbreak (slipstream), which allows the drafting rider to use about 20 percent less energy. Also called sitting in or wheelsucking.

Drivetrain: The components directly involved with making the rear wheel turn. Comprised of the chain, crankset, cassette or freewheel, and derailleurs. Also called the power train.

Drops: The lower part of a downturned handlebar typically found on a road bike. The curved portions are called the hooks.

Dualie: A bike with front and rear suspension. Short for "dual suspension."

E

Elastomer: A compressible, rubberlike material used to absorb shock in some suspension systems.

Electrolytes: Substances such as sodium, potassium, and chloride that are necessary for muscle contraction and maintenance of fluid levels.

Endo: To crash by going over the bike's handlebar. Short for "end over end."

Ergometer: A stationary, bicycle-like device with adjustable pedal resistance used in physiological testing or for indoor training.

F

Fartlek: A Swedish word meaning speed play, it is a training technique based on unstructured changes in pace and intensity. It can be used instead of timed or measured intervals.

Fat: In the diet, it is the most concentrated source of food energy, supplying 9 calories per gram. Stored fat provides about half the energy required for low-intensity exercise.

Fire road: A dirt or gravel road in the backcountry wide enough to allow access by emergency vehicles.

Fixed gear: A direct-drive setup using one chainring and one rear cog, as on a track bike. When the rear wheel turns so does the chain and crankset; coasting isn't possible.

G

Glutes: The gluteal muscles of the buttocks. They are key to pedaling power.

Glycogen: A fuel derived as glucose (sugar) from carbohydrate and stored in the muscles and liver. It's the primary energy source for high-intensity cycling. Reserves are normally depleted after about 2½ hours of riding.

Glycogen window: The period within an hour after exercise when depleted muscles are most receptive to restoring their glycogen content. By eating foods or drinking fluids rich in carbohydrate, energy stores and recovery are enhanced.

Gorp: Good ol' raisins and peanuts, a high-energy mix for nibbling during rides. Can also include nuts, seeds, M&Ms, or granola.

Granny gear: The lowest gear ratio, combining the small chainring with the largest cassette cog. It's mainly used for very steep climbs.

Granny ring: The smallest of the three chainrings on a triple crankset.

H

Hammer: To ride strongly in big gears.

Hamstrings: The muscles on the backs of the thighs, not well-developed by cycling.

Hardtail: A mountain bike with no rear suspension.

Headset: The parts at the top and bottom of the frame's head tube, into which the handlebar stem and fork are fitted.

Hybrid: A bike that combines features of road and mountain bikes. Also called a cross bike.

I

IMBA: International Mountain Bicycling Association, an organization dedicated to protecting and expanding trail access for mountain bikers.

Intervals: A structured method of training that alternates brief, hard efforts with short periods of easier riding for partial recovery.

J

Jam: A period of hard, fast riding.

Jump: A quick, hard acceleration.

L

Lactate threshold (LT): The exertion level beyond which the body can no longer produce energy aerobically, resulting in the buildup of lactic acid. This is marked by muscle fatigue, pain, and shallow, rapid breathing. Also called anaerobic threshold (AT).

Lactic acid: A substance formed during anaerobic metabolism when there is incomplete breakdown of glucose. It rapidly produces muscle fatigue and pain. Also called lactate.

LSD: Long, steady distance. A training technique that requires a firm aerobic pace for at least 2 hours.

M

Mass start: Events such as road races, cross-country races, and criteriums in which all contestants leave the starting line at the same time.

Max VO$_2$: The maximum amount of oxygen that can be consumed during all-out exertion. This is a key indicator of a person's potential in cycling and other aerobic sports. It's largely genetically determined but can be improved somewhat by training.

Metric century: A 100-kilometer ride (62 miles).

Mudguards: Fenders.

N

NORBA: National Off-Road Bicycling Association, the governing body of off-road racing in America. A division of USA Cycling.

O

Orthotics: Custom-made supports worn in shoes to help neutralize biomechanical imbalances in the feet or legs.

Overgear: Using a gear ratio that is too big for the terrain or the level of fitness.

Overtraining: Deep-seated fatigue, both physical and mental, caused by training at an intensity or volume too great for adaptation.

Oxygen debt: The amount of oxygen that must be consumed to pay back the deficit incurred by anaerobic exertion.

P

Paceline: A group formation in which each rider takes a turn breaking the wind at the front before pulling off, dropping to the rear position, and riding the others' draft until at the front once again.

Peloton: The main group of riders in a race. Also called the group, pack, field, or bunch.

Periodization: The process of dividing training into specific phases by weeks or months.

Pinch flat: An internal puncture marked by two small holes caused by the tube being squeezed against the rim. It results from riding into an object too hard for the air pressure in the tube. Also called a snakebite.

Portage: To lift and carry the bike, such as when crossing a stream, ditch, or ground too rocky to ride.

Power: The combination of speed and strength.

Preload: The adjustable spring tension in a suspension fork or rear shock. It determines how far the suspension compresses under body weight and how much travel remains to absorb impacts.

Presta: The narrow European-style valve found on some inner tubes. A small metal cap on its end must be unscrewed before air can enter or exit.

PSI: Abbreviation for "pounds per square inch." It's the unit of measure for tire inflation and air pressure in some suspensions.

Pull, pull through: Take a turn at the front of a paceline.

Q

Quadriceps: The large muscle in front of the thigh, the strength of which helps determine a cyclist's ability to pedal with power.

R

Reach: The combined length of a bike's top tube and stem, which determines the rider's distance to the handlebar.

Repetition: Each hard effort in an interval workout. Also, one complete movement in a weight-training exercise. "Rep" for short.

Resistance trainer: A stationary training device into which the bike is clamped. Pedaling resistance increases with pedaling speed to simulate actual riding. Also known as an indoor, wind, fluid, or mag trainer (the last three names derived from the fan, liquid, or magnet that creates resistance on the rear wheel).

Rollers: A treadmill-like indoor training device consisting of three or four long cylinders connected by belts. Both bike wheels roll on these cylinders so that balancing is much like actual riding.

S

Saddle sores: Skin problems in the crotch that develop from chafing caused by pedaling action. Sores can range from tender raw spots to boil-like lesions if infection occurs.

Sag wagon: A motor vehicle that follows a group of riders, carrying equipment and lending assistance in the event of difficulty. Also called the broom wagon.

Schrader: An inner tube valve identical to those found on car tires. A tiny plunger in the center of its opening must be depressed for air to enter or exit.

Set: In intervals or weight training, a specific number of repetitions.

Singletrack: A trail so narrow that two cyclists can't easily ride side by side, which makes passing difficult or impossible.

Snap: The ability to accelerate quickly.

Soft-pedal: To rotate the pedals without actually applying power.

Speed: The ability to accelerate quickly and maintain a very fast cadence for brief periods.

Speedwork: A general term for intervals and other high-velocity training, such as sprints and time trials.

Spin: To pedal at high cadence.

Stage race: A multiday event consisting of various types of races. The winner is the rider with the lowest elapsed time for all races (stages).

Straight block: A cassette with cogs that increase in size in one-tooth increments.

T

Take a flyer: To suddenly sprint away from a group.

Tempo: Fast riding at a brisk cadence.

Time trial (TT): A race against the clock in which individual riders start at set intervals and cannot give or receive a draft.

Tops: The part of a drop handlebar between the stem and the brake levers.

Travel: In suspensions, the maximum distance a fork or rear shock can compress.

Tubular: A lightweight tire that is glued to the wheel rim and has its tube sewn inside the casing. Also called a sew-up.

U

UCI: Union Cycliste Internationale, the world governing body of bicycle racing, headquartered in Geneva, Switzerland.

Unweight: The act of momentarily lightening the bike through a combination of body movement and position. It's integral to techniques such as wheelies, bunnyhops, and jumps.

Upshift: To shift to a higher gear, that is, a smaller cog or larger chainring.

USA Cycling: The umbrella organization for American bicycle racing. Affiliated with the UCI.

USCF: United States Cycling Federation, the governing body of road and track racing in America. A division of USA Cycling.

V

Velodrome: A banked track for bicycle racing.

W

Wheelie: To elevate the front wheel and ride on the rear wheel only. The opposite is called a nose wheelie.

Wheelsucker: Someone who drafts behind others but doesn't take a pull.

Windchill: The effect of air moving across the skin, making the temperature seem colder than it actually is. A cyclist creates a windchill even on a calm day, a situation that must be considered when dressing for winter rides.

Wind-up: Steady acceleration to an all-out effort.

Index

Underscored page references indicate boxed text.
Boldface references indicate illustrations or photographs.